First published by Warren Ratliff, 2022

Title: A Mind for Moving Forward – A Small Business Owner's Mindset Guide / Warren Ratliff.

ISBN: 978-0-6454473-0-9 (paperback)

ISBN: 978-0-6454473-1-6 (ebook)

Subject: Small business owner mindset.

Book design and layout by eMatti

Royalty-free images sourced from https://stock.adobe.com/au/

Printed and distributed by IngramSpark

Keywords:

Small business owner

Mindset

Business start up

Warren Ratliff

A MIND FOR MOVING FORWARD

A SMALL BUSINESS OWNER'S MINDSET GUIDE

BY

WARREN RATLIFF

ACKNOWLEDGEMENTS

I gratefully acknowledge those who supported me – my community and my core influencers – in the creation and presentation of this book.

To my wife Helen, my undying love and gratitude for supporting me every step of the way.

To my book editor and proofreader, Rosie Kovacs of OneStopWriter.com.au for fine tuning my grammar and spelling.

To my brand designer, Evelyne Matti of eMatti.com.au for keeping my company's branding consistent and professional and for designing the cover and layout of this book.

To the Coaching Tools Company, Your Future Now for their constant source of inspiration when creating infographics and more.

Contents

INTRODUCTION

Why am I writing this book?

This book is specifically for small business owners who've made the jump from a corporate or commercial job. They've left the associated safety net of a salary or wage and are keeping themselves in business. They're also providing a supporting foundation for the Australian economy through sheer numbers. Often on a wing and a prayer, they take on the world, one customer at a time. And they quickly learn that business, as in life, goes through stages.

For the first few months, they were filled with excitement and enthusiasm for the vision that they carried into the new business. Then, after an initial settling-in period that can be anywhere from three months to two years (or more), the business often seems to swallow them. The daily grind, red tape, dealing with (and employing) people, the relentless and often heart-breaking chase for new customers and sales. Not to mention the accounting, legals, operations, logistics and more.

And often, there's no one they can really talk to. To bounce ideas around with. To run options and issues and what-ifs through a logic test. Someone who's been there and done that, or who can see through the day to day and keep the owner focused objectively on the long-term vision.

I'm writing this book to help those who have started – and stalled. Those business owners and entrepreneurs who now sit back and wonder if they did the right thing. Or those who have seen fluctuations in motivation, activity, energy, and success. Those people who contemplate and tackle the daily grind whilst hanging stoically onto their original vision. Small business owners (including franchisees) who have no one to talk to at the top and who need to understand what's happening and if it's normal to feel how they feel.

Chart 1: Counts of Australian businesses measured by employment size as at June 2019

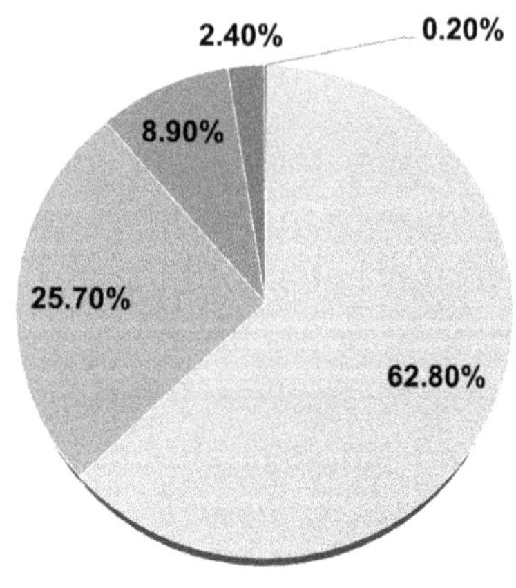

SOURCE: ABS Counts of Australian Business 8165.0 Table 13, Feb 2020 and ASBFEO calculations (excludes nano businesses)

Small businesses, including family enterprises, represent the lion's share of the overall Australian economy. According to the Small Business Counts Report of December 2020, over 90% contributed to the Australian economy in 2018 / 2019. And the number of small businesses swelled during the recent COVID-19 impact as larger organisations – the safety nets – shrank and people found themselves with no firm income.

So, in many ways, small business represents the heart and values that Australians hold dear. No one you will talk to doesn't know someone who owns, manages or works in a small business. By the way, in this book, small business is any organisation with less than 15 employees.

In 2020, small business employed over 4.7 million people. During the COVID-19 pandemic.

In Australia, 40% of small business owners are aged 45-59 years, with a further almost 33% aged 30-44 years. Over 19% of small business owners are over 60 years of age.

It's fair to say that, based on contribution and size, small business keeps Australia viable. It's like the engine room of the Australian economy. So feeling a sense of pride and passion towards small business is a form of patriotism. Caring for the country that we love includes caring for what makes the nation tick. And that includes caring for the owners and workers in the small business sector.

And that's where I come in.

With over 30 years of experience running and managing businesses in Sydney, the drivers, motivations, challenges, and successes that business owners go through are not lost on me.

Watching your sales and bank balance regularly crumble from forces out of your control can have an enormous impact on your mindset and willingness to keep pushing. Keep going.

Too many times, I've heard small business owners express feelings of isolation and worry. Knowing they'll have to make decisions about their lifestyle as they get older can make them anxious. And the choices, or specifically having the right choices available at the time, depend on the success of the business.

There is no lonelier place than the office of a small business owner when sales are down, margins are under pressure, staffing issues crop up, or marketing seems useless. Then there's delivery, logistics and administration. They can all be headaches for a small business owner that, without the right help and advice, can overwhelm the best operators and stop the business from progressing.

And that impacts on life.

I cut my teeth in small business, in a manufacturing environment. A 12 people-strong company where there were five directors in various functions, all of whom were hands on and involved at every level of the business. The business made and distributed niche products at a national scale across diverse markets. I started as a minor shareholder in office and administration management. Then I was forced, by necessity, to not only understand but to re-invent many processes to stay in tune with the technological revolution of the past 30 years.

Beyond that 15-year learning curve, I've held many titles: general manager, sales manager, CEO, director, franchisee, operations manager. But I found titles mean very little in small business because the buck stops with the owner. It's the owner who rolls up their sleeves and does whatever it takes to keep their particular ball rolling.

It's become apparent to me over time that titles in small business can present a hurdle for the business owner to achieve the growth they want. And need. Being prepared to do anything to achieve an outcome is an attitude that is almost a prerequisite for anyone considering starting or buying their own small business.

Over those years and hundreds of conversations with small business owners, I have realised that my journey was common for small business owners across Australia. The feeling of being alone at the top of the business. Of having no one to bounce ideas and thoughts with. Of having no one to hold me accountable to the actions needed to achieve growth.

Then, a short time ago, I did some self-development studies to facilitate my own (internal) continual improvement system. I began to understand and own my true values, belief system and real goals. This led to undertaking a lifelong journey to learn from every event (past and current) and this helped shaped my life. I applied those learnings to my goal to help other small business owners.

Everything I've done, achieved, suffered and endured in life and in business has led to where I am today. In my own business, coaching small business owners to develop their business and themselves.

And that is why I wrote this book. To put into ink (electronic or otherwise) just a few of the ideas and learnings that I've collected over the years and are relevant to every small business owner. Sharing a few nuggets of insight and experience to benefit those travelling the same (or similar) pathway through the rigours, rewards and challenges of small business ownership. As I did, and still do.

This is an interactive book. It includes several exercises and tools designed to help you understand yourself and overcome specific problems that you may face. You can choose to do the exercises, or not. It's up to you, as is life and the choices that you make every day.

Through the book, you'll see a few icons.

When you see this icon, there will be a short 'nugget' of gold information that might (or might not) offer an important point for you.

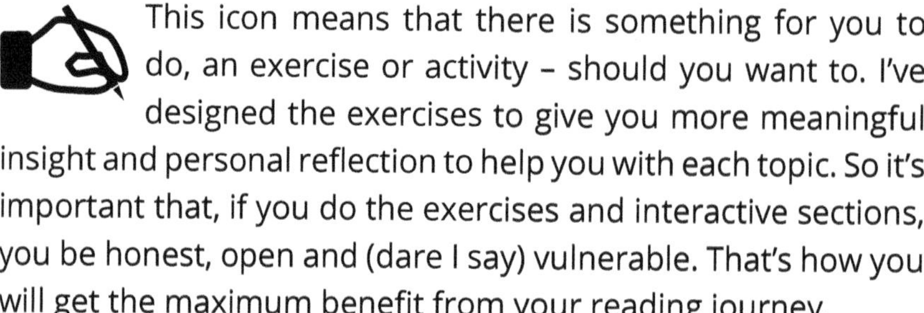

This icon means that there is something for you to do, an exercise or activity – should you want to. I've designed the exercises to give you more meaningful insight and personal reflection to help you with each topic. So it's important that, if you do the exercises and interactive sections, you be honest, open and (dare I say) vulnerable. That's how you will get the maximum benefit from your reading journey.

This icon indicates a few examples and case studies throughout the book to help you identify with the topic. Obviously, names and places are not included here, but I'd be happy to share more details if you wish.

Enjoy reading this book, and if you would like to contact me, you can reach me through my website: www.part3.com.au or look for me on LinkedIn, Facebook or Instagram.

CHAPTER 1: THE SMALL BUSINESS OWNER

REFLECTIONS AND INTROSPECTION

If there is one thing I've learned in my career, it is to do more of what's working, and less of what's not.

JIMMY WALES

When looking from the outside, running a small business can seem less hectic and complicated than what seems to be happening in a large-scale enterprise. But that view is relative. With supposedly fewer activities, less compartmentalisation, less employment and less large-scale works, the small business seems from the outside to be easier to manage. More reward for effort. More time to achieve. Live by the owner's standards.

But what goes into the process of starting and developing a small business to transform it into a successful enterprise? What is the secret sauce that takes business to the next level? Your own secret sauce that will bring clients and customers to you, rather than your competition. And how can you, the owner of the business, know every correct pathway and decision that will guarantee success? To make it pay and provide the lifestyle and income that you really want. It can be a struggle.

At the start of a small business life, it's only the business owner who feels the need to focus on all the activities and matters to get the business off the ground. Do this, create that, plan this. The owner can take a business forward with the right decisions and moves. Or, on the other edge, the business can be limited in growth to remain in that start-up size and scale. All subject to the approach and planning of the owner.

Either way, for a small business to keep growing, what should a business owner do? Is it only about strategies and best practices? Is it the industry? The timing of your venture? Your own skills and resourcefulness? Or is there something a little deeper that's common among all successful business owners that has been eluding you?

Starting your own business, as daunting as it can be, can really stretch you to areas where you are not comfortable. You're now a business owner. An entrepreneur. So think like one. Expand your skill set and your capabilities because there's a lot more to focus on for a business owner than there is for an employee. One major focus here is reflection.

It wouldn't be wrong to say that the owner's image shapes a small business's early days and years. A business image can be created by how the business owner acts, looks, feels. In this regard, when you plan to take a small business forward, your own self-reflection and willingness to accept change is a crucial step.

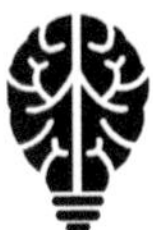

You can't change your small business if you aren't willing to change yourself. And the change you adopt will reflect in your business image.

Whilst every business owner and every business is unique, there exists in real time a commonality amongst small business start-ups that I've witnessed and heard about far too often:

1. First comes the dream. The vision. It's full of excitement and enthusiasm. Energy and action
2. Then the business starts. Steps are put into action and the dream becomes tangible
3. A few successes and wins put a little money in the bank. Great potential
4. It gets busier and the new business owner takes on some staff (at least one)
5. Growth plateaus and, with the added expense of staff, the pressure builds

6. The owner starts working harder – to bring in revenue and cut cost – at the expense of lifestyle
7. Pressure keeps building as the owner (and his or her family) works IN the business more to keep things moving
8. The owner starts thinking from the employee perspective – as a job – rather than as the entrepreneur – as a business person
9. The business seems to be going backwards, and the owner is responding to one crisis after another. The initial vision is greyed out and becomes background noise. They are not enjoying it anymore and their mindset leads to depression, anger, frustration, and anxiety

Sound familiar? Perhaps not for you, but do you know any business owners where this model may fit?

What is self-reflection in a small business?

> *'Self-reflection' is a reflective looking inward: an examination of one's own thoughts and feelings.*
>
> MERRIAM-WEBSTER DEFINITION

Whether yours is a small business or a large one, self-reflection (introspection) is a necessity. In larger enterprises, the self-reflection process may be more complex and involve several others, like operational staff and managers. However, in the early stages of a small business, it is crucial for the business owner to self-reflect and evaluate what changes need to be made – personally and to the business. They are all things to the fledgling business.

When it comes to self-reflection as a business owner, this includes asking yourself questions regarding how you work and how you think. In the early days (weeks, months), every business owner has some sort of plan set to achieve growth for the business. Your goals and objectives are set. Regardless of the size of the objectives, every strategy employed and action taken in the business is designed to progress the enterprise one step closer to it. Yet, often achieving that objective can seem impossible.

As time passes and you become more engrossed in the daily routine of your business, what tends to happen (a lot) is that the longer-term objectives drift into an intangible vision. Owners tend to find themselves working IN their business and less ON their business. Goals start to shift, and the lack of growth is somehow justified by the owner.

Great ways to really identify this is to either talk to an objective third party or, as we are discussing, self-reflect.

So, introspection plays a huge role for a small business owner. Looking internally and being totally honest and objective with yourself. This is where you take a moment to ask yourself questions and understand how you are working – and it can sometimes be very uncomfortable if done objectively. And it needs to be done regularly. Every business owner should determine if he/she is on the right track. Reflecting on your thinking, your work habits, lifestyle choices and approaches can help to better understand what you're doing well and what's maybe going wrong. Get your thinking in the right direction to benefit yourself AND the business.

To make a business image flourish in the eyes of stakeholders and potential customers, a business owner needs to be brutally honest in their self-reflection. And have the will to self-adopt change.

When we talk about the business owner and a small business, both go hand-in-hand in the reflection criteria. A business can reflect what the owner may be; the owner also reflects the image of a business. However, the only way to change business to improve it is for the owner to adapt with the change.

ACTIVITY 1: Daily self-reflection

Using the table below, reflect at least three times today and record any negative emotions you feel at the time – and what you did to overcome any negativity (if you did). Note down how you handled the negative emotions or thoughts.

If you had no negative thoughts, then use a positive emotion and describe how you used it to create an action.

Time of day	Emotion (What did you feel?)	Action (What did you do?)
Example: Waking up in the morning	Felt anxious about upcoming meeting	Read my meeting plan aloud to ensure I knew my material
Waking up & breakfast		
Lunchtime		
Just before finishing for the day		
After 'knock off' – the 'me' hours		
Any other 'emotional' time		

What are the challenges?

We talk of challenges, which is a positive mindset way to say problems. And challenges in self-reflection can heavily impact on our personal process for awareness. Looking inward objectively can be a scary prospect because you may not always like what you see. You may identify weak spots in your action plan or your language. I want you to reflect on the past two weeks. Can you honestly tell me there was nothing else you could have done in that time to step you forward in your vision? How much TV, Netflix and social media did you watch or participate in? Could some of that time be better spent on brainstorming, exercising, creating, reflecting and/or planning?

I ask people all the time, 'What has been your greatest challenge in the past week?' Then, as the conversation unfurls, the old chestnut words materialise: 'problem', 'try', 'if', 'but', 'however', (another word for but). Like Groundhog Day, the same patterns emerge – with some people more than others. People, business owners included, get stuck inside their comfort zone and become unwilling to persist as soon as they encounter any resistance. I hear the sentence, 'I tried to do XYZ, but the problem with that is if I do it ... blah ... blah'. Or 'I would have done XYZ, but the problem is I've tried it before and it didn't work.'

So, they didn't even try. Not really.

When previous events cause us to have negative emotions and thoughts, they can come to the surface in a new, similar situation. Our brain says, *'Oh No!! We've been here before, and it didn't work for us then. This will definitely be the same now!'*

That internal dialogue (language) is often negative. *'I can't', 'I won't', 'That won't work', 'It's not my fault'.* We are all a product of what has transpired in our lives up to this point in time. Our reactions to specific events and stimuli are driven by our feelings and thoughts around the original event. So, our brain will go into defence mode. Protect us from the potential negative of doing something that is outside our comfort zone to protect us from being disappointed or hurt again.

The human brain is wired to do whatever is the easiest thing for us. The 'least line of resistance'. So, when we are faced with resistance, we will, by default, tend towards the easy pathway – often the negative – because it's easier. We keep watching TV rather than get on the treadmill, or we don't call that new prospect because they will probably say no. We say, 'Don't worry about the inactivity – it's just that one day.'

It's often easier for many people, including business owners, to start justifying poor or flat performance of the business when times get a little tough. It's the economy. It's the weather. It's holiday season. The list goes on. There are plenty of external factors that can be blamed for poor (or average) performance. It's human nature to look for the easy explanation and lay blame, rather than looking for a solution.

When we start looking into ourselves, there can be a natural tendency to gloss over any negatives or imperfections that others may see clearly but are justifiable in our own eyes. A typical challenge for small business owners is to learn how to reflect honestly and objectively. Take a walk down the hall of mirrors and take a long, hard look at yourself. Understand and accept if and where any change is needed, then surrender to the process. After all, nothing changes without action. Most therapeutic processes start with the identification and acknowledgment of the problem. By looking inward objectively, rather than justify an action or decision, ask yourself how it could have been better. Ask yourself the simple question, 'Why?'

Are you stuck in your comfort zone and making decisions based on staying there?

There's a popular thread of thought and philosophy around forward progress, momentum, action, and personal growth. And there are many people who talk about being inside a comfort zone. Even more who refuse to leave the confines of their comfort zone. They ignore the real limitations of growth because of their unwillingness to actually do something new – something that feels uncomfortable.

> *The further you get away from yourself, the more challenging it is. Not to be in your comfort zone is great fun.*
>
> BENEDICT CUMBERBATCH

But not everyone wants to grow their business or themselves. Some people are quite happy to just plod along and enjoy what they have. And that's okay too.

Your comfort zone is where your subconscious mind defaults to – your internal autopilot. By staying safe, we are protecting ourselves. We are not risking what pleasures and rewards we currently satisfy by doing new things.

If you opt for a safe life, you will never know what it's like to win.

SIR RICHARD BRANSON

We have all, every single one of us, arrived at where we are right now by doing the things that we have done. Profound, huh?

The fact is, though, if you want to achieve something that you have not currently achieved, you need to do something other than what you've been doing so far. You need to step outside your comfort zone to enable growth in the direction that you want.

ACTIVITY 2: Know your comfort zone

Here's an exercise for you to do to look at your comfort zone.

It is not because things are difficult that we do not dare, it is because we do not dare that they are difficult.

UNKNOWN

Introduction

When we are in our own personal comfort zone, we're often on 'autopilot'. We can feel safe, secure, confident, relaxed – it's a comfortable place. The question is, is it time to step outside of your comfort zone?

Answer these questions to know where you rank on your comfort scale:

When was the last time you tried something NEW?	
How much are you learning RIGHT NOW?	
How much do you feel like you are growing RIGHT NOW?	

Do you feel you're DOING too much or not enough?	
When was the last time you took a RISK?	
Do you feel like it's time for a shift or a CHANGE?	

Where are you on your 'Comfort Scale'?

Use your gut feeling to place an 'X' on the line to represent how COMFORTABLE you are in your life right NOW.

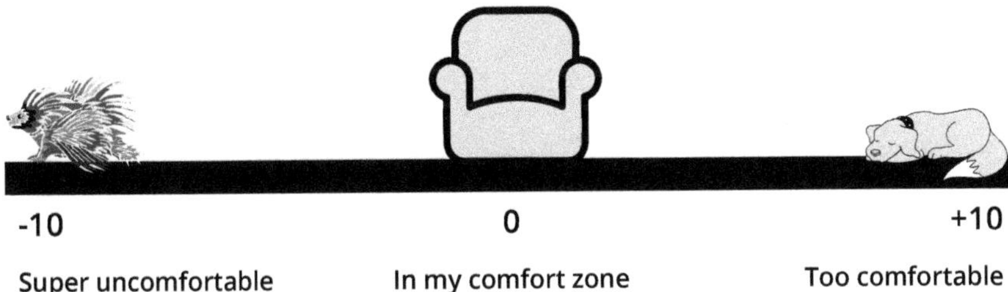

How is self-reflection by the owner going to help?

Remember, self-reflection and introspection are essentially the same thing. In your business, the process involves asking yourself questions regarding how you work and how you think. Self-reflection and objectivity are practices with which you may be unfamiliar or uncomfortable, particularly in the start-up phase. We tend to learn with experience as we graduate through our business stages and life. Through understanding and accepting our own personal Strengths, Weaknesses, Opportunities and Threats (S.W.O.T) – through analysis – our insights increase, and we're better equipped to maintain objectivity in introspection.

ACTIVITY 3: Objective self-reflection

These questions will get you thinking towards objective self-reflection.

Write down a 'DESIRED OBJECTIVE' that you're working on right now. It may be a project, a new client, a big sale or contract, or reducing costs. Or it may be personal. Then answer the questions to set priorities in your activity.

WHAT IS YOUR DESIRED OBJECTIVE?

____

____

____

1. What actions have you been doing that are STOPPING you from making it happen?

____

____

2. What actions have you NOT been doing that you need to START doing to make it happen?

____

____

3. What actions do you need to DO LESS of? (Less productive actions) to make it happen?

____

____

4. What actions do you need to DO MORE of? (More productive actions) to make it happen?

____

____

This exercise is a great way to reflect on how you spend time and how your time is allocated to things that yield varying degrees of productivity towards a goal. You can do this several times if you wish by using a different desired objective. And be careful not to eliminate an activity that you need for self-preservation. Many people find TV relaxing, and that's perfectly okay. So reflect on how much TV would feed your need.

For example, if you set the result as a weight-loss objective, reflect on how much time you spend sitting on the couch or peering into the refrigerator looking for the next snack. That time might be better allocated to raking the lawn or walking the dog (notice I avoided the 'going to the gym' cliché).

You may be doing some things that do not contribute at all to your objectives. What can you stop doing whilst maintaining a lifestyle? All things should be done or changed in moderation and change implemented at a manageable rate. If your form or relaxation is TV, then be careful that you don't eliminate your valued downtime. That might be better placed in the 'do less of' box.

Use this exercise in your personal life or your business.

The cycle of a start-up business mindset

Starting and initially setting up a business is exciting. And the mindset of the startup owner can be a different prospect to that of someone who is running an established business. A startup is often the consequence of a smart idea. A thought bubble telling you to break out of the nine-to-five. Be your own boss. Make money and create your perfect lifestyle. It takes passion, drive and motivation. It also takes an investment in time and money. And energy.

There's the creation of a startup business plan. Let's call it your business map. Your 'how to and when by' strategy. The plan will identify a customer need that, when satisfied, will enable a sale. The plan needs to have the flexibility to enable reactions to market and economic conditions, changes that could otherwise cause stress or negativity in the business owner. Your plan is a source for motivation as it contains the projected pathway to success, and how the growth will happen. It defines your perfect client(s). It is a map for business growth. And a business, just like an infant, needs to learn how to grow. The owner's ability and objectivity in self-reflection can accelerate or retard that growth.

Generally, there are various inputs and aspects of the owner's values, personality and skillset applied to achieve profit and growth. Through starting a regular process of self-reflection, the owner will be able to fine tune specific aspects of their input, and the activities within the business, to achieve outcomes. And that's an easier process when a good plan exists.

Through the start-up phase of business, when original strategies and activities tend to yield varying results, a pattern can emerge.

The owner needs to keep the passion and the motivation to continue the activities. Through results, they will see what works and what doesn't (in those specific times and conditions). And the process facilitates trying, learning, changing, and achieving. The process often involves some failures, so the mindset of the owner needs to be both strong and flexible enough to take the failures as learnings, make change and try again. Success comes with persistence in the right processes and areas.

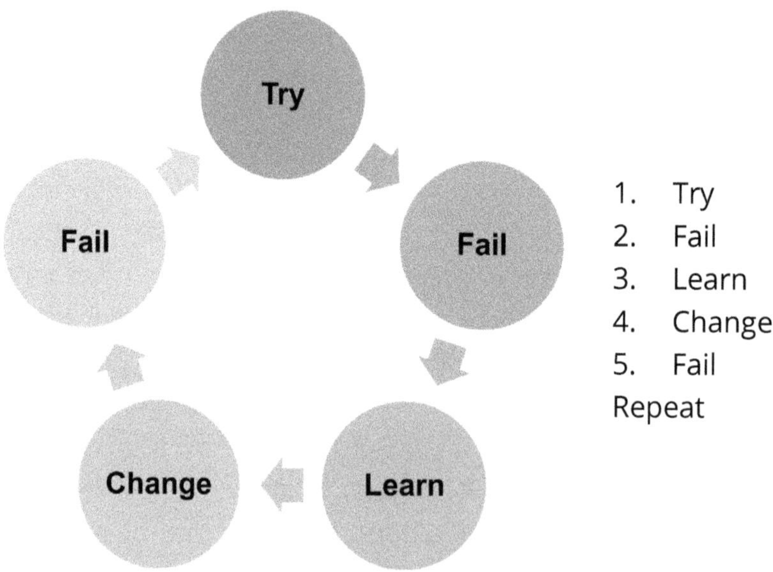

This learning process continues until a successful (sustainable) strategy rises to the surface.

Other environmental factors may also create a playing field for failures and learnings. These can include the ever-changing market, the economy, seasonal influences, worldwide pandemics, other players on your chessboard (competition), trends and your use of resources.

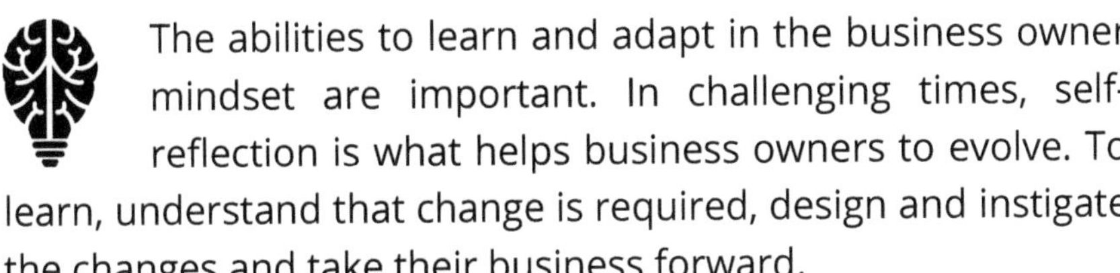

The abilities to learn and adapt in the business owner mindset are important. In challenging times, self-reflection is what helps business owners to evolve. To learn, understand that change is required, design and instigate the changes and take their business forward.

Business personality

We all have personality traits, with some more than others. How your personality traits reflect on the business is important self-realisation that can have an enormous impact on the success or failure of a business. In the planning stages, there will have been an image of the business, and specifically of you, the owner, IN the business. How you planned to feel, what you planned to be doing, how you were going to make your customers feel.

Ask yourself the question, *'Which of MY personality traits are reflected in the business, and how is that evident?'*

Think of WHO you are, as a person. Think of your reactions to other people. To external events that you can't control.

Are you:

- open to change (open-minded) or resistant of change?
- conscientious or passive?
- extraverted or introverted?
- agreeable or argumentative?
- easily depressed or resilient and happy?
- easily distracted or really focused?
- flamboyant or conservative?
- positive or tending to the negative?
- the life of the party or the wallflower?

We'll look at values later in this book, so for now, open your mind to the prospect of self-reflection and consider how your personality traits will present in the business. Then look at your market and your proposed clients and ask, objectively, how will THEY react to these personality traits? In what areas of business will they create a benefit or slow it down?

Self-doubt

For any business owner, self-doubt can be a common and potentially debilitating problem. Particularly when sales are soft, revenues are consequently down, and profit seems light-years away. Highs and lows are a part of every business. And in line with the reflection of the owner in the business, they may end up feeling like the business lows are just another symptom of their own personal loss.

Don't regret the past or fear the future.
Both bring misery through self-doubt.

DEEPAK CHOPRA

Self-reflection can, if mishandled, cause the owner's self-esteem to plummet. And a self-doubt cycle can make it seem like it's impossible to even identify, let alone get over, whatever is causing this downward phase. Objectivity becomes a victim of self-doubt. The owner can feel overwhelmed and believe it's impossible to achieve business success. At least in the short term. 'Impossible', however, is a word to be wary of when you are doing some self-reflection. It belongs in the negative language dictionary rather than in the positive language phrase book. Replace 'impossible' with 'how can I'.

Objectivity is key. Look inward and be prepared to own any negativity or negative language that you use and work out ways that you can make that language positive. If you do this regularly, you'll find that your language patterns and thought processes will automatically gravitate to the positive. This is a far more creative place for a startup business owner to be.

This principle applies to any business person at any stage of business. Being positive, whilst not the full solution, will put your mindset in a better place to tackle challenges.

For example, rather than saying, *"'It can't be done"... ask "How can I get it done?"* Rather than *"I'm too tired"* flip that to *"How can I get more energy?"* Change your language and flip the switch.

ACTIVITY 4: Negative language changer

Think back over the past couple of weeks and identify where you used negative language to either justify a poor result or as a defence mechanism. Write the negative language in the left column. Think how that language can be turned into a positive and write how you COULD have said it in the right column.

I've given you an example to get you going:

Negative language	Replacement positive language
Example: That won't work.	*How can I make that work*

Self-reflection driven change

It can truly be said that NOTHING changes without some form of action. And the action may have been initiated by you, the small business owner, the franchisee. Or, it may have come from an external source - your market, the franchisor, your staff, the economy, financial institutions, customers, suppliers, mother nature ... any number of places.

No matter what the problem is, it's always a people problem.

GERALD M. WEINBERG

What this means is that often we can't control change. It just happens. And then our reactions to the change will create further change. Action and reaction is often dictated by our self-reflection and internal belief system. Many people know from experience that change can be very stressful. Particularly if you did not initiate the change and you're effectively reacting. As much as we would like to, we can't control what we can't control (profound, huh?).

In a small business, change is almost inevitable and is often subject to the inertia (resistance to change) of the owner and their motivation. The fear response can be really stimulated if the change is not managed, controlled, in ourselves. It's often ignorance (not knowing how to handle the push for change) or this fear factor that prevents us from initiating any change in the first place.

It is wisely written (not by me, sadly) that whilst we cannot control what other people do and say, we CAN control our own reaction to the event or saying. We have the power to internalise and control our reactions. For the sake of our sanity, our reputation, our own mindset, self-confidence is a key part of managing change.

So adopt change, as long as it's controlled and progressive, and manage it with flexibility when the change is uncontrolled (like a COVID lockdown). Through introspection and awareness, control reactions. Manage the consequences of change, if possible, before it happens. Be pro-active AND re-active. If you put your mind to it, positive or productive change is possible.

What is productive change?

Think of productive change. A business owner's ability to identify and adapt productive change can help them develop in and with the business – and him or herself.

PRODUCTIVE CHANGE – DEFINITION

Productive change refers to altering states and circumstances to affect positive productivity and / or greater efficiency. Every action creates a change and every change creates a result. The efficiency with which a change creates positive results (that move you toward your goals and objectives) is the measure for productivity of change.

This may be a new concept for many 'old school' business owners. When we start out with the vision and the energy, we're all 10 feet tall and bullet-proof. Failure is not an option. Maintaining that mindset and applying it to yourself AND the business when times become challenging means self-awareness and changeability. So what change is productive, and what change is not?

When productivity refers to efficiency, productive change encompasses any change that leads, directly or indirectly, to an increase in efficiency.

When you self-reflect and identify that change is needed, remain in focus to evaluate the flow-on effect of any change you may contemplate. Is the prospective change direct or indirect? Will it create an immediate effect, a short-term effect or a permanent change? Will it step you and the business towards the pre-planned objectives? How will the change affect (and be received by) other people who may be involved?

From the outside, looking into a new business, you'll be able to see more clearly what might work and what probably won't work, if you can achieve a high level of objectivity (through self-reflection). The purity of right and wrong change approaches becomes clearer, as do the consequences and effects of planned changes. Positive versus negative effects. Knee-jerk reactions versus planned strategy. Well researched and thought through strategies will offer more chances of productive change, and that's what every business needs. It's a concept of how a business owner can better adopt a change in themselves and the business.

How can a small business owner adopt change?

At the risk of oversimplifying the answer, the small business owner can adopt change easier if they are prepared and ready for learnings. When they understand their own learning techniques. We looked earlier at the need for small business owners to learn and adapt as they try different ideas and endure different market conditions. The psychological process of gaining knowledge, including about oneself through self-reflection, varies with each and every one of us.

Yet we generally all fit into one (or usually two) learning techniques:

- Visual learners (I need to see it)
- Auditory learners (I like to hear or read about it)
- Kinesthetic learners (The touchy/feely learners)
- Auditory digital (Reading/writing learners – show me the evidence).

Adapting your internal learning type(s) to your self-reflection will help enormously when evaluating and planning future actions as a business owner. Once you understand the learnings of the past (or of other peoples' pasts), and you have drafted a change plan, it's often more controllable and comforting to start with small changes.

The objective of any change may be to step towards a huge goal. Trying to implement large change to reach the objective in one step can be not only difficult to do, but it may be damaging to you and the business. Small changes can create a steppingstone process to achieve larger goals. Then self-reflection at each point of change is a great barometer to gauge the effectiveness of the implemented change and make any course corrections as you go. Minor mistakes are easily rectified.

And since these minor changes require less effort and create less impact in business, lifestyle and resources, they tend to be less disastrous. As a result, a strategy of planning and implementing small changes can be the best approach to learn, understand and improve areas where you identify weak spots.

Often a business owner can achieve longevity in a business (sustainability) by implementing a series of planned and strategic small changes that will help step them towards a larger goal. Implementing small changes from time to time can be easily handled and adapted.

Problems that a business faces without a small change strategy

When we talk about how minor changes can be adopted and adapted in a business by the owner and the team, it's crucial to first understand what happens if the strategy is ignored. Often a small business owner's plan (before the start) fails to see that large decisions and pressure are a part of the game. Until you're in the ring, you can't tell how hard the punches are. However, it's not about the large decisions or work demands. Instead, it's about the small changes that you make in the business to make it grow further – to create long-lasting growth and sustainability.

Picture this. You want to make a 30% change to the business. That's a big jump. If, however, you implement a 5% change in one area of the business every month for six months (small changes), in six months you have a 30% change to that area of the business. And it was an easy transition. If you apply that to different areas of your business, you'll sell more and make more from each sale through increased efficiencies.

Without a strategy of small changes, a business can face:

- Reticence or procrastination to adopt large changes due to a sense of overwhelm or budget constraints
- Stagnancy - a lack of change and a static environment
- Limitations faced due to staying in the same spot – where the business started
- Lack of acceptance towards new ideas and staff in the business
- Inability to handle different and bigger clients
- Constant and greater failures
- Large flow-on repercussions
- Inertia from the increased fear of failure
- Large consequences that can affect every facet of operations
- Staff rebellion and loss.

Tips for adopting the right small changes

With the concept of implementing a series of small changes in self and business, it is often easier to evaluate the effects of the proposed changes than it would be if those changes were large scale. Self-reflection will help business owners understand where they need to go and take their business. The small adjustments to make along the way. But what about understanding the small changes needed to be considered for a business to achieve the larger goal? How do you set a series of milestones?

Small change concepts can be better understood and implemented with the following tips:

- **Evaluate business environment changes**: This is very crucial. Plenty of things can change in the business (or physical) environment for better or worse. To attain effective change outcomes, you need to keep an eye on the business environment factors and be proactive to forecasts and reactive to current events - all in incremental steps.
- **Accept potential results of change**: Before implementing change, the owner needs to accept what the change will bring. What it might mean for ALL affected people and entities. What will be the effect of a small price rise? What about a big price rise? We all need solid reasoning as to why change is necessary. Even in businesses, having an idea of the effects of a change is crucial.
- **Become an observer**: With any small changes you bring in for yourself and/or the business, there are repercussions to other people around you. This includes stakeholders, customers, staff, landlords, family members, and more. Contemplate others' reactions to the planned change. It may be worthwhile to take a consultative approach to understand if a change will be accepted by others.
- **Change your own thoughts**: How will you be successful and implement a planned change? How do you make change happen without changing your thinking? By changing the way you think, you will facilitate change by doing something different.

- **Look out for competition**: In the journey of adopting small changes, you're not the only one on the chessboard. Instead, there may be a lot of other business owners that are working on the same approach. It is very prudent to watch out for the competition. Be mindful, but not afraid of it.

Only with self-reflection can a business owner better understand who they need to be in the change, so they can help the business achieve the same 'ideal' objectives.

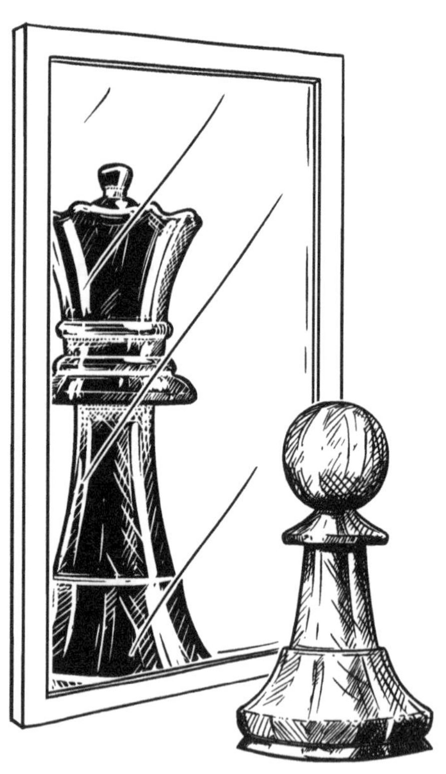

CHAPTER 2: MINDSET AND THE SMALL BUSINESS OWNER

When the vision is clear, the results will appear. Keep your mindset positive as you work your plan, flourish, and always remember why you started.

GERMANY KENT

indset is a term that many consider to be 'alternative' and a little outside of mainstream. Yet, it is a truly critical part of small business ownership.

Mindset:

- will facilitate the shape of future decisions and the implementation of past ones
- can mean the difference between success (growth) and failure
- controls how we feel at every moment and the impact that your current feelings can have on those around us

Your mindset can be one of growth, fixed, competitive, winning, positive, negative, sad, angry, hateful, loving, friendly... the list goes on and is not limited to simple emotional states.

In summary, it's a very important part of our lives that can shape how we make decisions. Your personal mindset will affect how you make decisions in life and business alike.

What is mindset?

In a nutshell, and at the risk of oversimplifying, here's my version:

> *It's a way of thinking. It's your collection of thoughts and beliefs that shape your thinking habits and attitudes. These then affect your choices and then your actions.*
>
> WARREN RATLIFF

Sounds simple?

Well, guess again. Your mindset is highly changeable, highly influenced by external sources, highly influenced by your internal beliefs and thoughts. It's these internal beliefs and thoughts that create your belief systems. Your thinking habits. And your belief systems affect how you think, what you feel, and what you do.

Your actions and reactions to different events, people, sights, places, and circumstances are driven by feelings that you hold internally. And your feelings are determined by your beliefs.

Shifting learnings

Since significant learning experiences have the power to change how we think about ourselves, relationships with others and perception of the world, changing the learnings in our mind around a significant event in the past can have a big impact on how we feel about similar events in the present.

WARREN RATLIFF

Your mindset impacts how you make sense of the world, and how you make sense of .... YOU.

Here are a few examples of general mindsets:

- An optimist's sunny perspective on life
- A business owner's entrepreneurial way of thinking
- An army general's military focus
- An elite athlete's winning mindset

A pessimist's glass half-empty perspective.

Sometimes, in places like clubs, committees or teams, a commonality of mindset spreads between people in the group and steers the entire group's outlook — psychologists call this groupthink.

There have been many articles, books, experts and strategists in the field of mindset. People have explored and researched the concept and as a result, there are several definitions of mindset, including:

- The Free Dictionary: A fixed mental attitude or disposition that predetermines a person's responses to and interpretations of situations

- Merriam-Webster.com - Medical Dictionary: A mental inclination, tendency or habit

- Vocabulary.com: A person's usual attitude or mental state is his or her mindset

- Cambridge Dictionary: A person's way of thinking and their opinions

- Dictionary.com: An attitude, disposition, or mood

- World English Dictionary: The ideas and attitudes with which a person approaches a situation, especially when these are seen as being difficult to alter

Whilst it can be difficult to identify the exact origins, some sources say the word mindset has been around since the 1920s. But I'm fairly sure that even cavemen had their own thoughts.

Here are a few experts:

- **Peter Gollwitzer** has written about mindsets since the 1980s (http://www.psych.nyu.edu/gollwitzer/).
- **Magoroh Maruyama** is famous for his Mindscape Theory. Mindscape is a construct from which coherent sets of behavioural mindsets can emerge. You can read more in *Mindsets and Science Theories* (http://heterogenistics.org/articles/Maruyama-Mindscapes_and_science_theories.pdf).
- **Carol S. Dweck, Ph.D.** popularised mindset when she went mainstream with her book, *Mindset: The New Psychology of Success: How We Can Learn to Fulfill Our Potential* (http://www.amazon.com/exec/obidos/ASIN/B000FCKPHG/thbosh-20/).

Carol Dweck, Professor of Psychology at Stanford University and one of the world's leading researchers on motivation and mindsets, theorised that there are two types of mindset – growth mindset and fixed mindset. What's the difference? I'm glad you asked.

A fixed mindset has people believing that their basic qualities, like their intelligence or talent, are simply fixed traits. They don't change as we learn and develop. Hence, these people would more likely document and record their intelligence or talent instead of developing them. They often also believe that talent alone creates success—without effort. Here's the rub – they're wrong.

A growth mindset is where people believe that their most basic abilities can be continually developed through dedication and hard work. The intelligence and talent are the starting point. People with this view are more likely to WANT to learn. They will have a resilience (learning from failure) that is essential for great accomplishment. Most people who are considered 'great' have had these qualities."

MINDSET ONLINE

As Dweck says,

> *Teaching a growth mindset creates motivation and productivity in the worlds of business, education and sports. It enhances relationships.*

So, what's your mindset right now, while you're reading this chapter? How does a small business owner use and control his or her mindset to benefit the business and their lifestyle?

> *What lies behind us and what lies before us are tiny matters compared to what lies within us.*
>
> HENRY STANLEY HASKINS

The entrepreneur mindset

As a rule of thumb, at the start of any business venture, the owner of the business, the entrepreneur, will have a GROWTH mindset. They will believe that they can improve, increase their mental performance, want to seek out new challenges and incorporate failure as a positive part of the learning and growth process.

When a business employs people, the team leader will heavily influence group thinking. In this case, the business owner. So, understanding the mindset of the team, the staff, stakeholders and family, and then leading from the front, is a key tool in extracting the most from the team. Encourage a mentality of growth mindset in their business. Encourage employees to challenge themselves whilst contributing to the growth of the business. Give them the feeling of ownership and autonomy (whilst you covertly maintain control) and allow them to learn inside a growth-oriented company culture. The positive growth mindset will spread, and the benefactor will be you, the owner, and all staff members.

ACTIVITY 5: Current mindset assessment

Here's a quick quiz to assess your current mindset.

1. Total and record your score for each of the 8 questions – record your total at the bottom
2. Interpret your score using the guide on the next page.
3. Total and record your score for each of the 8 questions – record your total at the bottom
4. Interpret your score using the guide on the next page.

	Mostly disagree	Disagree	Disagree a little	Agree a little	Agree	Mostly agree	SCORE
1. No matter how much intelligence you have, you can always change significantly	1	2	3	4	5	6	
2. You can learn new things, but you cannot really change your basic level of intelligence	6	5	4	3	2	1	
3.I like my work best when it makes me think hard	1	2	3	4	5	6	
4. I like my work best when I can do it really well without too much trouble	6	5	4	3	2	1	

	Mostly disagree	Disagree	Disagree a little	Agree a little	Agree	Mostly agree	SCORE
5. I like work that I'll learn from, even if I make a lot of mistakes	1	2	3	4	5	6	
6. I like my work best when I can do it perfectly without any mistakes	6	5	4	3	2	1	
7. When something is hard, it just makes me want to work on it more, not less	1	2	3	4	5	6	
8.To tell the truth, when I work hard, it makes me feel as though I'm not very smart	6	5	4	3	2	1	
						Total score	

Your total score is your current mindset.

Use the table on the next page to interpret your score.

Take the quiz weekly (or monthly) so you can track your mindset at different stages of your business and events in your personal life.

If your overall mindset score falls into this range ...	Then you usually believe the following things:
8–16	You strongly believe that your intelligence is fixed—it doesn't change much. If you can't perform perfectly, you would rather not do something. You think smart people don't have to work hard
17–24	You lean towards thinking that your intelligence doesn't change much. You prefer not to make mistakes if you can help it, and you also don't really like to put in a lot of work. You may think that learning should be easy
25–32	You're not sure whether you can change your intelligence. You care about your performance, and you also want to learn, but you don't really want to have to work too hard for it
33–40	You believe that your intelligence is something that you can increase. You care about learning, and you're willing to work hard. You want to do well, but you think it's more important to learn than to always perform well
41–48	You feel very sure that you can increase your intelligence by learning, and you like a challenge. You believe that the best way to learn is to work hard, and you believe that making mistakes is an inevitable part of the learning process

How to cultivate a growth mindset

Whenever you hear the experts talking about mindset, they're really talking about personal beliefs and how they can create blockages to achieving success and personal satisfaction. We've discussed a fixed mindset. Where the belief is that intelligence and talent are predetermined and set for life and unable to change in any meaningful way. As long as the person with a fixed mindset stays in their lane, improvement will just happen – if and when they want it.

Whereas a growth mindset involves the tendency to believe that growth is possible through hard and consistent work. Learnings are key and personal performance can improve with hard work. They overcome limiting beliefs by re-framing the original event and learning. And the learning continues as long as we do.

These two mindsets are present within most of us all the time. What drives our decisions and attitude in any instant will be determined by which is dominant at the time, and in what area of life.

Start in a job, finish with a business

Many small business owners in Australia have been in a 'job' previously. You probably started as a junior or a trainee, an apprentice or assistant. And there is absolutely nothing wrong with a long-term job as a career – IF that's what you truly want.

What is the difference between an ***'I have a job'*** mentality and ***'I have a business'*** mentality? At what point can we call ourselves an entrepreneur? What mindset should a new business owner have for the best chance of success? A **growth** mindset, or a **fixed** mindset?

Most of the important things in the world have been accomplished by people who have kept on trying when there seemed no hope at all.

DALE CARNEGIE, HENRY STANLEY HASKINS

As we discussed in Chapter 1, most small business owners start with a vision. They want to create something bigger than their job. Bigger than themselves. They want to get paid according to what they're worth (at least what they believe they are worth) rather than what's been mandated by a salary or wage for a defined role. So, leaving the job is a blessing. A cause for celebration. On the last day, they high five on the way out the door. All pumped up with anticipation and self-belief. They leave the comfort t levels of a job (and its pay) within an established business. They venture out and fend for themselves in the jungle of competition, pricing, marketing, sales, accounting, and every other part of small business ownership. Of course, this change can take a considerable shift in mindset, particularly when they start off on their own. First day, sit at the desk, switch on the laptop, make sure the monitor and internet are connected, check the empty email inbox, and swivel the office chair a few times. It's all good... it's only my first day (week/month). Plenty of time... I will build it, and they will come.... Right?

But many people at this stage struggle to make the required mindset adjustment. The growth mindset can be elusive. They quickly get dragged into the daily grind and ritual of things that must be done just to open the doors. The owner is the brains and the talent. But they need to go, mentally, from ***'having a job'*** to ***'owning a business.'***

How to overcome negativity and nurture a growth mindset

Below are a few things you can try to beat negativity:

- **Recognise and limit your fixed mindset:** Make time for reflection and get a grasp on who you are and what you're thinking. Acknowledge that you're stuck in a fixed mindset. It's the first step, right? If you're in a fixed mindset, you'll be sitting back waiting for success to come, because you have all the intelligence and talent that you need already. Recognise this trait through self-analysis (refer Chapter 1 – Self-reflection).
- **Acknowledge your weakness(es):** Do you stay in your comfort zone when challenging things need to be done? If you're not good at something, then see the weakness for what it is. By acknowledging weakness, we then take action to change. Then it becomes a strength. Learn about it or find someone who can.
- **Continual education:** As humans we never stop learning – as long as you WANT to learn. And if that's the case, then every day of your life will offer opportunities. Particularly with the access to information highways available through the internet. So rather than fight the learning, don't assume you know everything. Instead, adopt a yearning to learn.
- **Don't seek the approval of others:** Be your own driver. People with a fixed mindset spend too much valuable time

worrying about what other people think about them. Embrace a growth mindset by learning how to stop being concerned about what other people think and the perception that you are being seen as a failure. Stop worrying about getting others' approval. Instead, focus on your own development. Use this time to improve yourself for your own benefit.

- **Fail to succeed and succeed to fail:** Accept that failure is a part of learning and that it often takes a failure or two before you enjoy success. JK Rowlings tried 12 times before *Harry Potter* was introduced to *Bloomberry Publishing*. Embrace the failure and don't let the prospect of failure stop you. Be tenacious in the face of challenge and failure.
- **Invite and welcome challenges:** See them as opportunities for learning and progress. Don't look at the challenge as an obstacle. We will always face challenges. If you are not facing challenges, then you are static. If you are avoiding doing things because they are outside your comfort zone, even if they terrify you, they are the things that you need to do first.
- **Celebrate wins of others:** Celebrating a win of any magnitude is a great way to incentivise yourself to keep winning. And that goes for your team and people around you. Celebrate their victories with them. Empower them to want more. Spread the growth mindset across the whole team.
- **Accept and learn from criticism:** The feedback of others, when negative, is criticism. And that's okay. Because while you learn, you may not get it right every time. Without the criticism and feedback, how would you know? A great chef has different tastes than his patrons and relies on their feedback. You should also learn how to accept criticism and take on the learnings rather than dwell on the perceived failure.

A small business owner's mindset is often linked with the performance of the business. And a team, should there be one, will look to the owner for their own mindset. A growth mindset in the owner will be contagious.

So, how does the mindset of an owner change in concert with the business performance?

In crisis

When the business is in lean times, sales are soft, profit is down, and leads are thin. The owner can often shrink and go into defensive mode. Exude a deepening sadness that will creep into every corner of the business and its people. They might look to cut spending, worry about the future, worry about the team. It's not just a negative mindset – it's survivalism.

When this type of crisis hits, it's critical that the owner has some mechanism to drag themselves from the mental mire and think strategically and positively. Rebuild a growth mindset.

Feeling trapped inside a failing business will have potentially serious repercussions on mindset and mental health.

According to Forbes.com four areas are detrimental to mental health in entrepreneurs with failing businesses:

- **Impulsivity:** The owner will tend to react with a 'knee-jerk' rather than thinking of long-term consequences
- **Depression:** This can have significant and far-reaching effects on health, relationships, wealth and decisions
- **Social isolation:** The feeling of unworthiness or embarrassment can create an isolationist mindset that will deepen without active change

- **Humiliation, rejection and failure:** Business is largely about relationships, and yet it can be difficult to create and maintain relationships

Until the business (and consequently its owner) faces a crisis, they often feel procrastination and unwillingness to change. The business owner often will not act until they are in the grip of a crisis.

Don't wait until it's too late to call in the cavalry. Have the courage to ask for help BEFORE your business gets to crisis point. Foresee your future (as it will be on your current pathway) and create change when it's needed.

Negative mindset

Henry Fonda wrote:

> *If you think you can or you think you can't, you're right.*

Negative emotions

DEFINITION OF A NEGATIVE MINDSET

A negative mindset focuses on what might go wrong, rather than what might go right. It is a pessimistic way of thinking that will dwell on potential flaws, create worry and potential stress.

A major contributor to a negative mindset is what we call limiting decisions and negative emotions. We touched on these in Chapter 1.

We are a product of what has happened in our lives before now. And how we think about different things (people, events, circumstances, and happenings) is largely determined by our belief system, which is a product of our experiences and values.

You can't change your past. But you can certainly learn from it!

Reactive negative emotions that affect our mindset today are often caused by a decision that we have made in our past, at a conscious or subconscious level. Something happened, someone said something, some action occurred that led to a change, and we decided how we interpreted that change. How we felt about it. That interpretation created a feeling around that event. And created a belief.

We decided to feel the way we did about that change or event (or person). We refer to that decision as a limiting decision. It limits our belief system so that whenever a similar event occurs now, our feelings are determined by what happened in the past and how we felt about it back then.

A client of mine, a business owner, was telling me one day that whenever he visited a client site, he would always get into an argument (heated) with the car park attendant. He believed every car park attendant was 'out to get him'. He was a victim. We explored this and uncovered the first time he remembered this happening several years ago, and from that

point, it seemed like the norm. He got riled up at the very thought of car park attendants.

We went back to the first time he noticed this happening. Why did he think the attendant reacted in the way he did? What made my client react as he did? What were the possible reasons behind both reactions that he never considered? A powerful question to ask here is, 'What were the learnings from this situation?' My client realised it was his attitude that was causing the car park attendants to react with a perceived aggression. Generally, the answers here are powerful enough to change the mindset to a positive and empowering position.

To simplify, identify the FIRST time you felt a negative emotion about the event. Then work with someone to change the way you feel about whatever caused it. You'll find you can change your mindset very quickly.

Your thought process around these events can be changed by redefining the event's meaning. Re-framing the event to make it a learning experience (retrospectively) can change the way you think of the same event when it happens again.

Similarly, a positive mind will view a goal or objective with more clarity and focus. We can make greater achievements with a growth and positive mindset. People around you will thrive, problems turn into challenges and success is a far more common result. Adoption of positivity is a great way to keep looking to the future with the right attitude. There are many books and publications written about positive mindset and handling everyday problems (challenges) with ease. And the end of this chapter will provide you with some very simple processes to help you 'turn that frown upside down'.

For a small business to succeed, a small business owner must adopt a positive mindset. A growth mindset.

What are some effects of a negative mindset?

A negative mindset in a business owner can mean a great chance that the business may not grow effectively – or even fail. Some of the negative effects this mindset can cause include:

- Limited creativity
- Limited vision and planning ability
- Inability to learn and grow professionally
- Lack of business growth
- The inability for the owner to work with the business team as a TEAM
- Customer dissatisfaction or lost clients
- Disgruntled team members
- A negative image of the company/business
- Stagnation
- Inability to convert leads to revenue

More simple ways to shift a personal negative mindset into a positive mindset

There are many ways to shift your mindset. As we saw earlier in this chapter, developing and cultivating a growth mindset takes a little effort but is well worthwhile. There are industries and businesses built upon the shoulders of positivity and mindset shift.

Positive mental attitude is a concept originally introduced in 1937 by Napoleon Hill in the book Think and Grow Rich. As old as it is, this book, and its concept, continues to be relevant. It is recommended reading, discussing the importance of positive thinking as a contributing factor of success.

Rather than read a plethora of books and self-help guides, following are a few more simple things that you can do to shift to a positive mindset:

- **Move:** The quickest and simplest way to break a negative state is to move. Do a few star jumps (I know, sounds like exercise), do a jig, a dance, wave your arms, go for a walk. Just move. Because physiology and mindset are very closely related. Often when we are in a negative mindset, we stay still, stuck in a negative thought cycle. Sharp and dramatic movement will usually break the negative state and allow you to think clearer.
- **Think 'big picture':** Reflect on the vision(s) you had for yourself when owning your business was still a dream. Why did you start in the first place? What is your TRUE goal? Through looking at the bigger picture, the little things that cause frustration will become smaller and less stressful.
- **Identify your values:** Align yourself with your top five values. Our values help to determine our belief patterns. Extract and prioritise your top values so that you can truly understand yourself and what drives you.

- **Create (or look at) a vision board for your perfect life:** A visual montage with goals and ideals. Have them written, using bright imagery for the pictures and placed where you can see them easily - every day. A good vision board will motivate you every time you look at it.
- **Create an anchor:** Anchoring is a good way to get yourself 'in state' whenever you want. Installing an anchor can enable you to instantly, and at will, change to the state that you want. Perhaps a salesperson wants to feel a state of confidence and power walking into a big meeting. Or a teacher wants to install a state of calm authority before going into class. Anchoring is a powerful tool when done properly.
- **Stop comparing yourself to others:** Be your own advisor. Don't get drawn into vanity and aesthetic comparisons with others. Live by your own standard and be proud of who you are.
- **Talk to a coach or mentor:** A good coach or mentor can lift you from your fog, your mire. Before you engage a coach, though, read the last chapter in this book.
- **Take a little time for yourself:** Schedule some 'me time' for yourself. We need to take breaks now and then to keep operating at peak performance. Even supercars need a pit stop, right? Take a break every few months. Meditate. Do whatever you need to recharge and refresh. Go see a movie on your own if that works for you.
- **Meditate:** The idea of meditation is to clear your mind. This is a very personal and private thing to do. Some people get most meditation benefit whilst walking. Some need total

silence and a comfy chair. Some might listen to music. All of them are okay. As long as you can establish calmness and self-awareness to reflect in your most comfortable way.

- **Do a little breathing exercise:** We need to breathe to survive. So, no shock that oxygenating ourselves helps to stimulate calmness and clarity of thought. Here are a couple of techniques that I've found useful:
  - 7-11 (In through your nose for 7. Out through your mouth for 11) or,
  - 7 x 7 x 7 x 7 (in for 7 through the nose; hold for 7; out for 7 through the mouth; hold for 7; do this 7 times)
- **Actively permit yourself to think positively:** Recognise the symptoms of negative thought, of fixed mindset, and focus on changing to a positive one. We ALL feel negative at times. It's natural. Accept it and create your own process to get back into positivity as soon as possible. That's where the magic will happen.
- **Do a random act of kindness:** Pay for the coffee of the person in line behind you. Buy a Big Mac and give it to a homeless person. Help an old person across the street. Buy some cookies and give them to a neighbour. Compliment someone on how they look. It's easy to put a smile on someone else's face – and that smile WILL BE contagious.

A small business owner can make the business's shape and image turn into reality with a positive mindset. Anything can be achieved when you can learn to think and act with positivity. In any business, large or small, this mindset that comes from the top down can, and will, play a huge part in success.

Elite sports people approach every moment during a match or game as if they have already won. It's merely a matter of time and ensuring that the pieces fall into place the way they pictured them – and mentally rehearsed them – then victory is assured.

CHAPTER 3: PROCRASTINATION AND DECISION MAKING

Procrastination is the fear of success.

DENIS WAITLEY

I want you to reflect for a moment and be really honest with yourself. Be objective. Have you ever had to make a decision or take an action that you put off as long as possible? Or avoided completely? For whatever reason, there was something (usually fear) stopping you from facing the decision until the critical (very last) moment – if you faced it at all. There's no shame here, by the way. It's natural. At some point in their life, most people have faced this delaying tactic. It's called... you guessed it... procrastination.

WHAT IS PROCRASTINATION?

Procrastination is the act of delaying or putting off tasks and / or decisions until the last minute, or past their deadline. Research has found that it is often a form of self-regulation and has been linked to perfectionism, feelings of inability and lack of self-confidence.

So, what can it do to a business if the owner of the business struggles to make uncomfortable decisions and take action in a timely manner?

The fact is that procrastination is an issue we all face from time to time. Whether you are a student, a parent, an entrepreneur or a professional businessman, procrastination will affect your performance and abilities.

Who is most affected by procrastination and why? Is a specific type of job more impacted by procrastination than another? Is it purely an individual thing and why has it become an issue? Can anyone face it at any time? How can you get past it?

When a person moves from having a job to owning a small business, they face plenty of new responsibilities. It comes with the territory of entrepreneurship. These new responsibilities mean that they need to make decisions that, until now, were not even thought of. Sure, having a job brings many responsibilities too, but you always know that someone has your back. You are not where the buck stops. Real issues can get passed up the food chain to your boss (who might just pass it back to you and make your life hell). Often you may bask in the knowledge that you are a mere cog in a giant wheel. Someone else is responsible for making the business work and succeed. You have KPIs or sales numbers to meet that, once met, make your life easier because you've done all that was required of you at that time.

However, when you start a small business, the responsibilities and working criteria change significantly. Suddenly, you have a greater risk if you make a bad move. The responsibility is different. As a business owner, you have to check everyone's performance, especially your own. You need to make sure everyone's work is focused on giving your business the best chance of success.

Often you are called upon to make a snap decision across all areas of the business. The increased responsibility and the need to make fast and fluid decisions can impact you. Suddenly faced with the daunting prospect of failure, procrastination can set in. Consequently, the shift in your thought process will reflect on the team, clients, prospects, suppliers, and your inner circle (family and friends).

Whenyou'renotreadytohandleincreasedresponsibility, it often results in procrastination. When a person shifts from a job to a small business, he or she often faces the natural fear or anxiety around business decisions. As a result, procrastination can be common among new business owners who underestimate the magnitude of their responsibilities on their journey.

How does procrastination hurt a business?

Let's be clear. Not everyone faces the issues of procrastination when they start a business – or at any time, for that matter. And it's not necessarily an ongoing trait. It can happen to people at any time, even if they've never felt it before. It's a situational thing for many people- brought on by new situations, changes, emotions or a number of other factors.

Its repercussions for the small business operator can impact far more than themselves. It impacts on every part of their life, their family and their business – whether startup or established. So it's something to be on the watch for. Be aware – not afraid.

It's important to understand the root cause of any procrastination and realise whether it's a common trait when the owner experiences any type of change. Is procrastination, for example, a common trait in other areas of their life?

To get to the roots of procrastination, to understand its causes, it's worthwhile to get some insight into the owner's decisions and decision-making processes. It helps to be able to look into the past to identify any historical event or emotion that may be responsible. Did something occur in the past that determined the owner's belief system and has transformed into procrastination now?

If the owner cannot make decisions or manage the decisions he or she takes on the run, procrastination is certainly going to have some form of impact on the business. A prospect asks for a better price. A supplier wants to increase your costs. A client wants to visit your premises. So many things can act as a trigger for the owner that will, if delayed or avoided, potentially cause damage.

I once worked with a wholesaling and service providing business as their general manager. Sales and business development were my main functions. We had a remote owner/director who wanted every quote to follow a specific template, and every high-ticket quote to be passed through him before they went to the client. Of course, clients tend to want things now, right? The additional time it took for him to proofread every quote and tender and then massage the pricing was time that belonged to the client (not us). It continually made me question if our priorities were aligned. He was a procrastinator – and his inaction impacted my ability to convert a client.

What this combination created was a sales quoting environment where quotes were regularly delivered late and tenders were submitted after the close date. This caused the conversion rate to plummet, as the clients were not prepared to wait for the director to get the last 't' crossed. The consequence, naturally, was a challenging top line because sales went to competitors.

How else can procrastination hurt a business?

There are multiple ways a business can be easily shaken:

- It can lead to **lack of confidence** in making decisions. Especially if the business is a one-man-band solopreneur with no support network
- It can cause a **lack of productivity** in the workplace and employees. The owner won't make a call, therefore neither will the team. Everything grinds to a snail's pace and lead times are in jeopardy
- It can **ruin a business's ability to meet deadlines** and maintain relationships with clients. It impacts your reputation and the chance for referrals. Customers like to feel important, like they are your ONLY customer. Reaction times can impact that belief
- It can **create apathy** among the team where everyone believes they have more time to act. Inefficiency is a consequence
- It can lead to **missed opportunities for sales** and consequent growth. If the owner can't respond to a tender or quotation before the opposition – well, you snooze, you lose
- It can **negatively impact your health**. Recent studies show that putting things off (procrastinating) can lead to increased stress. And the associated negativity can lead to illness

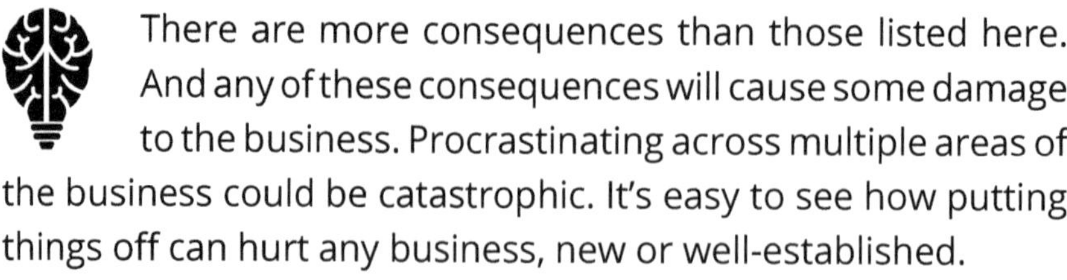

There are more consequences than those listed here. And any of these consequences will cause some damage to the business. Procrastinating across multiple areas of the business could be catastrophic. It's easy to see how putting things off can hurt any business, new or well-established.

Decision making for a business owner

When it comes to making decisions, we all have different ways of handling this. And there's no right or wrong way to make appropriate, timely and effective decisions. It's truly up to each individual to create their own reactive and fluid decision-making process, where their belief systems allow them to make the decision in their own way. And, I hate to say, there will be mistakes along the way. It's called – wait for it – being human.

> *Take time to deliberate; but when the time for action arrives, stop thinking and go in.*
>
> NAPOLEON BONAPARTE

In business. a decision is often based around a set of options. Should we do this? Or should we do that? However, looking for and uncovering those options can be tricky for many business owners, let alone choosing the best one. The fact is that there is ALWAYS an option. You may not like several or all of the choices, but there will always be options. The very fact that you need to make a decision is because there is an option. Do this or do that. Approaching a problem or challenge with limited options can make the decision-making process seem uncomfortable as you try to fathom the best option to take.

Why decisions fail (Paul C Nutt – 2002)

Paul Nutt is a management sciences and public policy professor in Ohio State University's College of Business. In 2002, he originally published his book entitled, *'Why Decisions Fail'*, in which he explored reasons for the failure of decisions made in business. His theories claim there is a core of three common blunders that generate seven traps that then lead to bad decisions.

Here is a summary of his premise:

The main idea is that to make better decisions and avoid the debacles – those costly wrong decisions which end up becoming public knowledge – you need to avoid the three blunders. And these are present in all debacles. Then you can avoid the seven traps which can lead to bad decisions.

The three blunders are:

1. **Rushing to judgement** – before all the requisite information is at hand
2. **Misusing resources** – thereby squandering the opportunity to apply those resources more intelligently
3. **Consistently applying failure-prone tactics** rather than best practice tactics

These blunders in turn generate seven traps which can collectively or individually underpin bad decisions. The seven traps are:

1. **Seizing the first idea that comes to mind** – even if it doesn't quite fit the circumstances
2. **Ignoring potential problems and barriers** – and ploughing ahead in the belief everything can be sorted out at a later stage
3. **Failing to specify clear-cut objectives** – thereby allowing ambiguity to dilute organisational effectiveness

4. **Being unwilling to look for better ideas** and approaches than those already in use
5. **Being selective in the collection and analysis of information** - and only emphasising the data which supports the decision
6. **Leaving ethical questions in the background** - to be sorted out later rather than sooner
7. **Ignoring the opportunity to learn from previous mistakes** - and making the same mistakes over and over

It is a quirk of human nature that, for some reason, many decision makers consistently apply the tactics which have a poor track record of success. The simple act of replacing the widely adopted error-prone tactics with better tactics that avoid these seven traps would increase the chance of success by as much as 50%.

Research shows that half of the decisions made in business and related organisations fail. The true failure rate may be higher because failed decisions that avoid a public airing are apt to be covered up. Considering the vast sums spent on these decisions and the benefits forgone, finding ways to avoid failure is vital.

PAUL NUTT

In further research, Paul Nutt found that the frequency of bad decisions reduced significantly by adding options. Simply by adding one option and creating a good, better, best scenario (or poor, okay, good), the failure rate dropped to around 30%. Obviously, in an efficient decision-making process, the addition of too many options could again lead to procrastination, as it takes too much effort to evaluate the options. But by increasing the choices beyond the yes or no, do this or do that, you can make your process easier and more efficient.

Analysis paralysis

I often see people in business make decisions first and then worry about the consequences afterward. A wrecking ball approach. Easier to ask forgiveness than it is to ask for permission. And then there are plenty of other people who do the exact opposite. They worry, and think, then think of something else to worry about.... before they make a decision. IF they make it at all. They suffer from analysis paralysis.

It's surprising that both these ways of making decisions tend to work from time to time for different people. What's also interesting is that even the greatest procrastinators are capable of making very quick decisions. It would be prudent NOT to step in front of a moving bus – right? Yet the procrastinator and the anticipator (the opposite of procrastinator) will make the same decision every time. Self-preservation trumps over-thinking.

> *In a moment of decision, the best thing you can do is the right thing to do, the next best thing is the wrong thing, and the worst thing you can do is nothing.*
>
> THEODORE ROOSEVELT

If you're running from a hungry lion, you won't stop to think about what colour shoes you should have on. You'll just run.

The individuality in the decision-making process helps divide us from the rest of the animal kingdom. And it can absolutely make a difference between gaining success or facing failure.

So, back to the business owner. If the owner delays making a decision, they may miss opportunities. They may fail to react to market demands or external influences. They may affect the performance of the entire team. They may lose clients, respect and reputation. They may develop an illness.

For example, look at a tender process. There is normally a finite time frame for response submissions, and sometimes that's not much time. The business owner may procrastinate to the point where it's impossible to complete the work in the remaining timeframe. He may take the attitude, 'Next time... I'll get the next one'.

Getting around procrastination

If you are still wondering if YOU are a procrastinator, check your email inbox or the tray on your desk. Ask your friends, family and staff. We discussed self-reflection in Chapter 1. The identification of procrastination in yourself can be a real light-bulb moment. Wow... I do tend to put things off that make me a little uncomfortable. Changing, on the other hand, can be a long-haul process.

If you procrastinate when faced with a big difficult problem... break the problem into parts, and handle one part at a time.

ROBERT COLLIER

A business owner needs to understand and implement possible methods and tools to stop procrastination. Some simple tools, processes and steps can be enough for a business to succeed in this quest.

These steps can include:

- **Replace thoughts that are stopping you** with goal and task-oriented thoughts that inspire you. The process here is to record and list the dysfunctional thoughts as they come up, then record an appropriate rational response
- **Remember your vision** when you started. Remember the new owner high fiving on his way out of the office on his last day at 'work'. That vision probably didn't factor in any delays caused by procrastination
- **Recognise that you are procrastinating.** It's the first step in most rehabs – recognise that there is a problem
- **Understand WHY** you are procrastinating. Is it fear, self-doubt, disorganisation, inexperience, perfectionism? Then take steps to change whatever is the root cause. Get external help to dig out the root cause, change your beliefs around that and move you forward
- **Back yourself and your abilities.** You started this venture with passion, drive and a thought. Back yourself. Ask yourself, *"If I knew that I could not fail – what would I do?"*

- **Focus on DOING**, not avoiding. All change starts with an action
- **Ask someone to check up on you.** Keep yourself accountable
- **Set goals** and break them down into small daily actions. Eat your elephant one bite at a time
- **Reframe your internal negative dialogue** – 'I will', rather than 'I'll try'. Here's another gem: 'There is no try. There is do, or do not.' (Yoda – for you Star Wars buffs)
- **Reward yourself for positive actions.** Celebrate the wins, even if they are small
- **Keep (and keep to) a daily 'to-do' list.** Change it daily or even hourly, if need be, to stay fluid
- **Schedule time** in your calendar for activities where you might procrastinate
- **Put yourself in the shoes of someone you really admire** when you feel yourself putting something off, and think from their perspective. What would THEY do right now?

Letting go of procrastination can lead to exhilaration and success. Find your own way to let it go. Stay present and focused, and learn about your own belief systems.

Be open
Be proactive
Be true to yourself
BE YOU

CHAPTER 4: MOTIVATION AND ACTION

There's no shortage of remarkable ideas, what's missing is the will to execute them.

SETH GODIN

Have you ever been instantly impressed at someone's energy levels or noticed a lack of drive? Some people seem to fill the room with intangible energy when they enter. Some can build it progressively through their communication style, tonality, vitality. While some, ... well, all the energy seems to get sucked out of the room. Energy, of course, is not motivation. One can lead to the other. And I've found that high energy people are more motivated.

Over the course of my career, I've had the privilege to meet and speak to literally thousands of business people, workers, solopreneurs, coaches, trainers and motivators. And one constant amongst all of them is change. Changes with their mindset, energy levels and, particularly, motivation. Even the most upbeat person at times suffers from de-motivation.

Motivation is a mindset. As such, it can be shifted and massaged around by good practice. It will also be subject to wild fluctuation.

In brief terms, motivation has ultimately only two types. **Toward** motivation, and (you guessed it) **Away** motivation. You may prefer **Carrot or Stick** motivation. What's the difference and how does that impact you, the small business owner?

'Toward' motivation (the carrot) motivates people towards a reward. When you are motivated to progress in the direction of something. You hold a carrot out for a horse to motivate the horse to come to you. Say, for example, you really want ice cream. Your motivation to go to the shop to buy it is toward motivation. You are heading in that direction because that is the way to get your ice cream. This is focusing on the possibilities and vision of what you want.

'Away' motivation (the stick), on the other hand, is when you are motivated away from risk or pain. You are motivated to avoid it. You make decisions and act away from what you don't want. You don't want to break your healthy eating diet, so you are motivated NOT to go to the shop. You put the car keys back in the drawer on purpose, so you don't go to the shop. You are motivated by what you don't want, so you act accordingly.

What is your motivation at work? The carrot? Or the stick?

WHAT IS MOTIVATION?

Motivation is a driving factor for what actions we take in the present. It dictates willingness to create an action in accordance with immediate, short-term and long-term goals.

Motivation is one of the most important reasons to move forward. Motivation results from the interaction of both conscious and unconscious factors.

I was with a small business owner recently in his retail business in Northwest Sydney. When I asked, 'What do you really want?' He started with, 'Well, I don't want to be losing all my clients because of price.' His answer was quick, and he didn't need to think too hard to come out with it.

But he didn't answer my question. It's easier for us to dwell on the away motivators than it is to recognise the toward motivators. By answering with what he doesn't want, it took a little more time to drill into what he really wants. And when he realised his own patterns, I'm sure I saw a little light come on.

When I was working as a general manager for a wholesale and industrial service business, my service person was offered a range of incentives to build business with serviced clients. There were KPIs set in place and there were occasions where he went outside his boundaries and needed to be pulled in. Unfortunately, the stick, or away motivators, that were employed for him did not work. He simply shrugged his shoulders and went on doing whatever he wanted. The most effective incentive by far was the toward motivation of additional pay and bonuses for client services and building business.

In business, the stick approach rarely works. The stick usually presents a threat and, as a consequence, people will often react negatively. People like to feel empowered, not threatened. The carrot will usually empower by offering a reward for achievement.

Action against motivation

For a small business owner, it's easy to lose sight of how you can achieve something, especially if you don't have the motivation or dedication to finish it. Whether it's a personal or professional task, motivation is needed to keep working on something until it is completed. Often, for a number of reasons, we lose interest. One minute you are full of it (so to speak) and then it's gone. And the change can be caused by a huge number of factors: environmental, physical, spiritual, or the actions of others. In terms of health, a lack of motivation can cause laziness or low energy. Since laziness is quite common, lacking enthusiasm is also equally common and recurring. However, that may not be the only reason you lack motivation in life.

Go back and think of times when you were assigned a task or job, but it took you hours to complete it – if you completed it at all. Or remember when you doubled down on your effort and felt frustrated when the results didn't improve at the same rate as your effort. You may have questioned why you bother. The frustration you felt created a lack of motivation. And that's often from a lack of interest caused by the perception that others are putting you down. We are more motivated to achieve things in which we are interested, and this indifference prevents us from completing a task.

The small business owner can lose motivation through a huge range of factors and variables that are often outside of our control:

- Fear of failure
- Avoidance of difficult conversations or tough tasks

- Actions and attitudes of other people
- Personal perception
- Lack of preparation
- Low self-confidence
- Perfectionism
- Lack of reward or positive acknowledgement of achievements (e.g. a simple thank you)

These factors can create a barrier to taking your business further.

Motivation is a complex concept in terms of what it means to YOU and your business. It has the power to lift your life and career to high levels. Or it can demolish a business and your life achievements step by painful step. Whatever the reasons may be, without the right incentive and putting steps in place to maintain and manage the motivation, it's difficult to achieve success in your business. And, let's face it, for a business owner that usually comes down to money.

In a business environment, there is a continual threat to which the owner of the business will fight as a response. And the fight may mean some emotional and mental injuries and hurt along the way. These are learning experiences – not failures. And your motivation needs to be fuelled by not only the learnings but also the heady prospects of success.

However, you don't often instantly lose motivation. Especially when you are a sole owner of a small business, you know that only your efforts will take this business forward. Therefore, even when your business leads and sales dwindle, a business owner's motivation drives him or her to keep working hard and do more towards marketing and selling the products. That's the only way your diminishing revenue can start rising, right? Once your pipeline strengthens again, you can shift the business focus towards delivering the products or services to the clients.

Focus on one thing at a time, and do it with high and continual motivation. Maintain the vision. See things through from start to completion.

Relationship between motivation and action

Motivation is an intangible thing that shifts in intensity in line with our actions and environment. Whilst you can't touch motivation, whilst it has no tangible physiology, it is real. And it can be likened in some ways to the old conundrum, 'What came first, the chicken or the egg?' Did you act a certain way because you were motivated? Or were you motivated because you acted a certain way?

Both these questions can be answered with a resounding YES. Every action is preceded by motivation. Then what happens once you've done that specific action? Change happens. Then your motivation to do something else will take over and cause you to act again. To RE-ACT.

Think of a boxer. A boxer is motivated to win a fight contest by hitting the opponent. The long-term goal may be to win an Olympic gold medal. The medium-term goal is to win the next contest. During the contest, the short-term motivation is to hit (and to avoid

being hit). Once you land a blow, then you are motivated to move (so you don't get hit back). And then a cycle is set in motion where you hit, move, hit again. Each time you hit, it's because you see an opening. You are motivated by the opening and throw a punch. A small action. But you don't stop there. Each action is predicated by another singular motivation. And the long-term goal of winning the gold medal is still there – motivating.

Motivation is fluid. And it changes all the time, steering and guiding whatever immediate action you do. Then, once you have done one action, you're immediately motivated to do another action. And the motivation changes. But regardless of immediate (in the moment) goal or short-term motivation, your long-term goal hangs in there, driving all other motivation. And it is that larger goal that creates a gap into which we will be motivated to step. To act. To close the gap.

To achieve large goals, smaller objectives would normally be set in place. Milestones. The boxer had to hit, and avoiding being hit, as a short-term goal, and winning the next bout as a medium-term goal. That contest is a milestone. An action step.

By setting achievable action steps that will, when done, step you towards your larger goal, your motivation at that moment (in that action) moves you towards your larger goal.

Say you want to lose 20kg in three months. Your goal is clear and set. You need to start walking or running, but you need a new pair of running shoes. Your long-term goal is to lose the weight. Your short-term milestone is to get in the car, go to the shop to buy the shoes. (Then you see the donut shop and ... well, you get the picture.)

Your short-term motivation (to buy shoes) directly aligns with your long-term goal (to lose the weight). So achieving the milestone of new shoes is (pardon the pun) a shoe in. You act accordingly. Grab the keys. Go to the shop. Try on the shoes, and so on.

Then, with brand new shoes on board, you go for a long, brisk walk. Your action towards the long-term goal has also satisfied the milestone.

Action and motivation are closely linked. Every action is predicated by SOME form of motivation.

The actions that you take have a direct consequence on your immediate motivation. The completion of an action right now is caused by an immediate desire to carry out that action. By ensuring that our small actions are aligned with a larger goal, there is, by default, a better chance of attaining the larger goal faster. Your motivation, goal(s) and actions are aligned.

> *People often say that motivation doesn't last. Well, neither does bathing – that's why we recommend it daily.*
>
> ZIG ZIGLAR

With motivation, life and business collide. Action, or more specifically the consequence of action, has a significant effect on your immediate motivation. Various factors, including money, can be the major incentives in running a business. When money or any other factor drives you to build your business and keep working on it, you take action to step towards success despite the possibility of lows and failures. Your goals, actions and motivation are aligned.

And the same alignment needs to happen in business as it does with the business owner's personal life - in most any other area of life. Be specific when you set goals. And make them motivating. The goal needs to get you to ACT.

A recent client initially stated his goal to be a comfortable retirement. On further questioning his motivations for retirement, the focus shifted from the word 'retirement' to the word 'choices'. His ultimate motivation was for him and his partner of many years to have choices. Money was a driver for the choices. A motivator. His goal morphed into having financial security (money) to allow the choice of continuing to work, selling the business, or running the business passively through a manager. When we identified the true goal – choices – his motivation increased five-fold, which then led to planned and strategic actions. The result? After three months, he is on target to have his choices available within two years.

We'll look at goal setting in Chapter 6, so stay tuned.

The motivational roots of a startup

Motivation is at the root of any business startup. Think back to when you started or bought the business in which you now find yourself. Then, ask yourself what motivated you to buy or start the business in the first place.

It probably stemmed from a vision, a values alignment, or a unique opportunity. Perhaps it was an 'away' motivation – you really had to get away from your old boss and starting your own thing seemed a great option. Or was it a towards motivation (maybe you always wanted to run your own business)?

The owner is highly motivated at the start. And the high motivation levels will endure for varying periods – subject to the owner, the environment, early successes, early failures, and surrounding influences (Chapter 5).

People become entrepreneurs for their own reasons, their own motivations, including:

- Generating wealth: providing for a family and financial security
- A vision of transforming people's lives: they want to make a difference. Leave the world a better place
- Autonomy: be their own boss and go it alone
- A sense of accomplishment: sit back in later years and look at what they've created

When the going gets tough

Picture the motivation levels and intensity for a new business owner. In the early days, all staff, friends, the family are supportive, and everything is zinging along. Then things get a little tighter. Money tends not to flow as naturally as you planned. It's taking a little longer to get to profit and you start to feel a little 'stuck' IN the business. You wonder how long the 'push' marketing will go for until you reach critical mass, and the market begins contacting you.

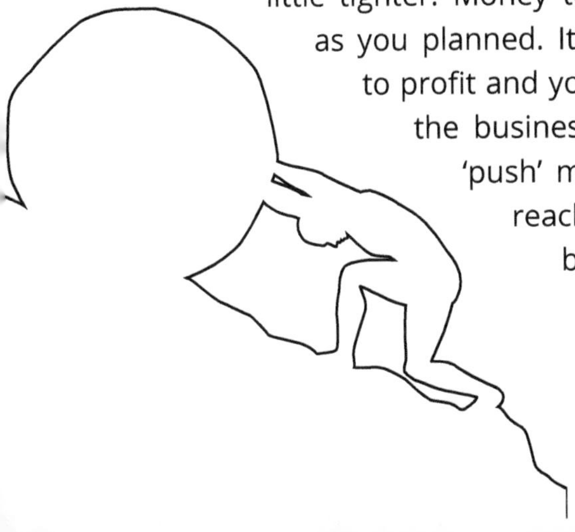

Your initial high motivation wobbles a little. The big picture is still there but the small stuff, the daily grind, starts to eat away at you. It's a very common occurrence. And you often don't see yourself as being stuck until a crisis happens, and by then it's sometimes too late. Your motivation towards your larger goal (whatever that is) and your actions will change when you lose the 'big picture' motivation.

At times like these, a business owner can stop performing in their business. Motivation wanes, activity (the right activity) stops, and the energy in the business falls away. The business owner might spend less time on the business and more time avoiding it – by doing anything that's not business related. Perhaps time is now spent watching YouTube or streaming TV shows more than you used to. When this happens, the owner will often lose sight of their original vision and that's where the feeling of being stuck happens. They can't see the forest for the trees. The team (if there is one) will be affected as the owner can go into depression and their mindset can go into survival mode.

The tough get focused

Every business (and its owner) faces its ups and downs. During the tougher times, how do you lift mindset and your business from its low to take it towards its high? The business owner needs a mindset shift to stay focused and start (or continue) looking at the bigger picture. Keep their eyes on the prize and re-focus. They need to remember WHY they are in the business, WHO they are doing it for, and WHAT the desired result is. This will enable motivation to increase again and the business will start to move ahead.

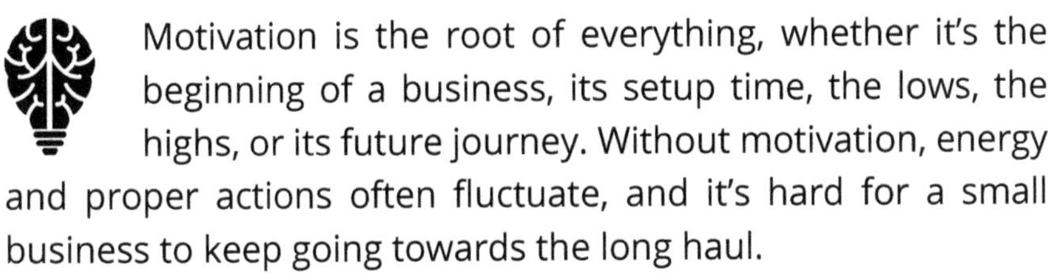

Motivation is the root of everything, whether it's the beginning of a business, its setup time, the lows, the highs, or its future journey. Without motivation, energy and proper actions often fluctuate, and it's hard for a small business to keep going towards the long haul.

ACTIVITY 6: Self-motivation assessment

HOW MOTIVATED ARE YOU?

This quick quiz will give you an idea of how motivated you are currently.

INSTRUCTIONS: : Think about your business goals, then answer the questions by selecting the response CLOSEST to how you feel in your life today. The answer you select is just an indicator – there are no right or wrong answers.

1. Can you visualise or imagine the benefits of these goals for YOU?
   a. Yes, I can clearly see/hear/imagine/feel the rewards I will get by achieving my goals
   b. I know what the benefits might be, but I can't quite imagine achieving them
   c. No, I find it hard to imagine things being different

2. How prepared are you to make changes to your life to achieve your goals?
   a. I'm ready to do whatever I need to do to make it happen
   b. I'd like to see how much I can achieve; I'm pretty busy but am ready to make some effort
   c. I'm not ready to make big changes yet; I have too much going on to change much
3. How passionate are you about achieving your goals?
   a. Absolutely, I want it more than anything else right now
   b. I want to get there – but at my own pace
   c. A little; If I can make a small change, I will be happy

4. Are you prepared to get the right support with planning and executing your goals?
   a. I would love support in specific areas (e.g. brainstorming; action planning; identifying obstacles; accountability)
   b. Some support is good; If I make a plan, I am more likely to stick to it
   c. I'm not ready to change so don't need support at this stage; I prefer to work on my own

5. Do you persevere? How much willpower do you have?
   a. When I set my mind to do something, I achieve it
   b. It varies. I have good days, but sometimes life gets in the way; I get distracted or tempted off-track
   c. Not much. I have often given up in the past because of a lack of willpower or commitment

Your scores

	A	B	C
TOTALS			

Your motivation quiz results

MOSTLY As – THE BIG LEAP

You are highly-motivated, organised, determined and keen to make changes.

You will achieve your goals one way or another, and if you don't there's always a very good reason.

Make sure that you don't forget to celebrate and enjoy the accomplishment of milestones and small victories. Or let other things in your life slip as you drive towards your goal. Sometimes your focus can block other things out.

MOSTLY Bs – THE MIDDLE WAY

When a goal is big and important enough, you take action. But like most people, you occasionally struggle to stay focused and motivated. You have a full life and probably know what works for you (and what doesn't), but are you set in your ways? Your motivation may vary as you're unsure how change would fit into your life. This means that sometimes you just let things happen around you (and to you) rather than actively creating the life you want

Life and work is predictable and safe (even if busy). You mostly feel settled and may have what you feel is a good 'work / life balance'.

It's easy to get nice and settled in your comfort zone. But you might also take longer to achieve your goals because you don't have the strongest of motivation, clarity, organisation, energy or support you need to go the extra mile.

MOSTLY Cs – SMALL STEPS

Perhaps you're happy with your life and your goals are simply a fine-tuning exercise

Perhaps you're not really enjoying your life and are struggling to get moving on your goals. Maybe you can't see the benefits of your goals enough. Maybe your life is simply too busy and overwhelming or maybe you've been going after the wrong goals

Small steps are the perfect way to hone and shape your life and start working on your goals. Set small goals as milestones. Change rarely happens overnight and taking it slow lets you fit change into a super busy life.

Summary of challenges for a business lacking motivation

Problems can arise if a business owner and/or the team lacks motivation. The desire to take the right actions, at the right times, to run a business and actively market its products. These problems or effects of lack of motivation can include:

- Declining revenues (sales)
- Poor pipelines: the future revenue generator
- A 'desperation' or break-even mentality: settling for just okay
- High staff and team turnover: staff can be motivated to leave you
- Low employee and customer engagement: customers will be drawn to a more positive supplier
- Poor communication among the team, customers and stakeholders

- Diminished productivity
- Poor health: a wide range of health and physiological negative effects

It's a cycle

The motivation/action cycle is one that every small business owner should understand. This chapter has detailed how motivation can vary in an instant and how keeping a vision of your larger goals is important to keep motivated. We've discussed how every action is predicated by some form of instant motivation. Then change happens from the action and the result of the change will impact on the next motivation.

Here is the cycle:

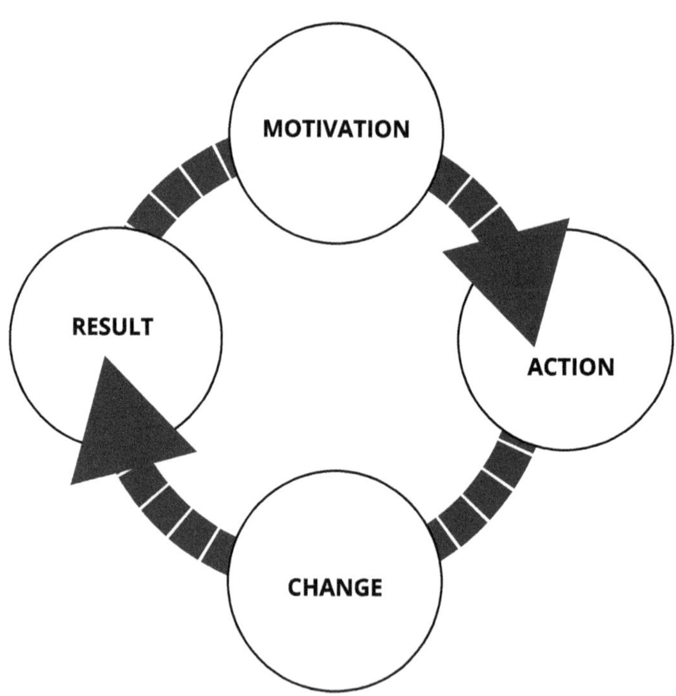

Simple techniques to maintain or reclaim your motivation

You can actively take steps to maintain motivation through a range of tools:

- **Remember the big picture.** Your vision. Create and display a vision board with everything that you dream of. Seven years is a good timeline for a vision board
- **Think of the WHY.** Not the WHAT. Why did you start this in the first place? If you keep reminding yourself of WHY you are doing something, the action will align with your values, which, in turn, will align with your goals
- **Practise gratitude.** Write down three things for which you are grateful right now. Do this every day, or at least whenever you experience some negativity, and watch your motivation come back
- **Identify your true ideals** and align your values. Goals and visions that don't match your values are destined for under-achievement. Of course, it's important to know yourself, your real (silhouette) values, so that you can recognise alignment
- **Anchor a positive mindset state.** Go from a negative state to a positive state through an action or process that works for you
- **Recognise and deal with obstacles.** As they occur
- **Create a major goal.** A big, hairy, audacious goal to control all others (yes – like the Lord of the Rings)
- **Create a daily action task list.** To keep moving towards major goals – daily / weekly / hourly

- **Always finish what you start.** And celebrate when you finish something successfully
- **Get help.** Support from friends, family, coach, mentor, colleagues, or other business owners. Accepting help is NOT a sign of weakness
- **Reconcile yourself with failure.** It is a rehearsal for success – a learning curve
- **Identify and face fears.** Whatever they are in business, including fear of failure
- **Dream your vision for the future.** Allow yourself to dream. Many people feel dreams are intangible, so they don't allow themselves to believe in a dream or vision of the future. Guess what? You're allowed! Motivate yourself by asking what your future COULD be – like your dream
- **Surrender to the process of growth.** Allow yourself to feel and act
- **Identify and change bad habits.** Self-awareness and reflection will identify them. Only you can change them
- **Be prepared to change.** Embrace it and own it
- **Be in awe of something or someone.** Sometimes life feels like it's just one action after another. When and what did you last wonder or marvel at? And who do you admire?
- **Images can be powerful.** Think of a symbol, object or word that represents your goal and INSPIRES you (e.g. role model, glossy fruit bowl, mountain, animal). What qualities does

your object have that you'd like more of? Now put a picture somewhere you will see it regularly (e.g. car, computer screen, mirror, wallet, fridge door etc) for regular inspiration

- **Get to know yourself.** Start a journal and record what motivates you (or doesn't) during your day, and give them a score: __ /10. Review and notice the activities, patterns and habits that boost, and get in the way of, your success!

Motivation is one of the six keys to success

When you have the vision, set the right goals and maintain motivation; then take action, accept change and become accountable – you will enjoy SUCCESS.

WARREN RATLIFF

If you have VISION and GOALS

You need Accountability

If you have GOALS and MOTIVATION

Nothing happens without Change

If you have MOTIVATION and VISION

You will take Action

CHAPTER 5: THE IMPACT OF YOUR PEERS

WIND BENEATH YOUR WINGS OR DEADLY DOWNDRAFT?

"I don't like the word 'dynasty,' but that's what it is. It's not just a business. There's a lot going on in the background."

JAKE DYSON

Family and friends are usually the most important support system in our life, particularly in our early life when we are developing our values, beliefs and behavioural patterns. We need permission to do... well... anything! As we age, our needs mature. Our support system morphs from mum and dad or parental figures into friends and colleagues. Peer group pressure changes to a need to conform–with society, community and business standards demanding a thing called 'responsibility' (ugh).

INFLUENCE

The power to have an important effect on someone or something. If someone influences someone else, they are changing a person or thing in an indirect but important way.

Think for a moment on who it is in your life who has, over time and experience, exerted the most influence on you. In your past, perhaps when growing up as a kid, a teenager, in college. Perhaps in your work life. And, of course, the present. Who has been (and is) close enough to make a difference to you? These influencers help create you. Who you are, what you are, what you believe, and what you do.

Look at your five closest friends. Those five friends are who you are. If you don't like who you are then you know what you have to do.

WILL SMITH

Our peers and surrounding influences create a deep effect on us. They can create the framework of support and direction for our lives. There is a natural familiarity amongst the group because they are of similar mind to yourself. There are often different groups within your sphere of influence, and they may or may not know each other. Your tennis club members may, for example, not know anyone in your football club. Yet they are both a part of your surrounding influences.

And ironically, you may not have met many of your influencers. You may be so inspired and influenced by someone that their characteristics and traits exert a magnet-like effect on you. Or your groups may be online through a social media portal. When thinking of your influencers, think outside your everyday sphere of known associates and relatives.

I asked a recent client who was influencing them in life and business. The question was to name three people who he really admires. The three came easily, and one of them was Neil Armstrong (for those under a rock – the first man to walk on the moon). His business is growing steadily (my client's – not Neil's) because he is now thinking of business decisions in the context of 'What would Neil do?' He's never met Neil Armstrong, yet the influence he's having is quite profound.

It's important to differentiate between the different types of influences (and influencers) that impact our lives. This will change as we grow – in age and in business. They change with the intensity and type of influence they have on you. And your influencers are not always positive. They are not always aligned with your personal vision and goals. In this case, the influencers can become a deadly downdraft rather than the wind beneath your wings.

Among your influencers will be your **core influencers**. Your close friends. Family. Normally long-term, close associations you confide in at a personal and vulnerable level.

There will also be your **personal community – your tribe**. Usually more in number, your supporters, fans, detractors are people you surround yourself with your own tribe. These people are in your life, but not as close as your core. Those with a similar mindset and vision will support you, whilst detractors will be your devil's advocate.

Core influencers – Close, stable, nurturing

Who they are

- Family
- Close friends
- Coaches
- Mentors
- Teachers (at the time of study)
- Your boss(es)
- Smaller group – often individuals

Who they influence

- The influence is comparatively intense and often sets a standard or value to which you will measure yourself
- Your belief systems and feelings can be determined by these influencers
- There may be a permissive type of relationship where you seek the approval of these people prior to doing an action or making a decision
- Regardless of your actions and performance, this group would normally be there in the same relationship before AND after any actions or decisions
- Negative feedback will not change the relationship
- Core influencers tend to be very supportive and believe in you, and want to see you succeed. This level of influence is huge for the business owner - on self-confidence and motivation

Personal community (tribe) – Removed, like-minded, independent, come and go

Who they are:

- Social groups
- Work colleagues
- Networking groups
- Workgroups
- Friends (not AS close)
- Social media friends and groups

- Neighbours
- Sporting teams and groups
- Competitors
- Study groups

What they influence

- Larger group and may comprise several groups with different commonality of interest
- Will 'like' what you do (or not)
- Relatively 'low impact' influence where an opinion may be valued but not necessarily agreed with
- Specific to the nature of the group, the influence can be varied (i.e. the tennis club may influence your tennis game)
- Negative feedback may disrupt the relationship
- People will come and go from this community

To demonstrate, let's say that you were contemplating starting your own business. You have the drive, the passion, the vision. You're excited! Then you talk to your family and friends about it and they effectively shut you down. Maybe a few support you, but others don't, for whatever reason.

Then you approach your personal community. You ask them for some market research and the feedback comes back positive. 'Go for it', was the collective encouragement.

So, what to do? Do you push on regardless and create your own business, risking potential alienation of your core influencers, knowing that they will still be there regardless of your decision?

Or do you shelve the idea and stay in your current job – effectively having been put back in your box?

Your core surrounding influencers, given the nature of your relationship with them, will still be there in support of you personally, because that's the relationship. If you fail, they'll still be there in support. The relationship is different from that of the personal community.

On the other hand, because they are not as close, your personal community can influence you at an ongoing and motivational level. There's an aloofness to the relationship(s) in these groups that every person takes differently. We've learnt how important motivation is to your success. And the sphere of influence (from influencers) can have a big impact on your motivation.

Today our community, our tribe, comprises not only people we've met personally, but indirect contacts through electronic and online media from far and wide. And the level of influence can also vary, although there is an element of maturity and emotional intelligence in how much we are influenced at the different levels. Teenagers, for example, are often heavily influenced by social media feeds of people who they have not, and never will, meet in person. Among a flood of positive comments, it can be the one negative comment that destroys the motivation of the vulnerable.

Your surrounding influences directly and profoundly affect how you think, feel, act, and perform. Your surrounding influences are critical for your success.

Build me up – or tear me down

Let's say for a moment that you are playing tennis. You've been playing for around 12 months so you can handle yourself on the court. You really want to improve, so you join a group to play tennis every few days for practice. These are your new community. New members of your tribe. They have come into your personal sphere of influence because of a change that resulted from your action in joining the tennis club.

Then you discover that the playing group you joined has only beginners for members. No-one has more experience nor greater skills than you. They are all just starting out on their journey. You win every game easily at first. But you find the games get a little harder and you stop trying. Your skill level is dropping while your opponents' skills are improving the more you play with each other. And then you find over time your game has not improved. Rather, it's either stayed the same or gone backwards whilst your teammates' skills have improved.

Now imagine the same situation, but this time your group has only players that are better and more experienced than you – some significantly so. You really struggle to win a game initially, so you keep trying harder. The others give you tips and help with your game. You play the same number of games as in the first (beginners) group, only now your game is improving. Your skills are higher, and your fitness is better.

The only variance here is the experience and skillset of the other people in the respective groups. The community.

When you surround yourself with people who are levels above where you are now, and in a similar or affiliated field, then their achievements will 'pull' you along. Your own game, business, actions, thoughts, and motivations will change as a result. Their thoughts toward you will grow along with your interactions and successes.

Surround yourself with those who only lift you higher.

OPRAH WINFREY

How do you associate with a community of successful people with a similar mindset and will effectively pull you towards success? Particularly in business, where competitors might already enjoy the success to which you aspire?

The key lies in the concept of 'collaboration' rather than 'competition'. Reach out to people who play in the same sandbox – but not necessarily with the same toys. Identify your own niche, area of expertise, your specific offering. Then research others who have accomplished success in the same client type, yet in a different niche. They may be in the same industry and at a different level. They may be in a place to which you aspire.

Through association with these surrounding influences, your own game will improve. Your motivation will stay true and on target.

Without the support and encouragement of the people around you, any tough times and challenges at the start become harder. Association with high achievers, mentors, mastermind groups and coaches will provide specific influences that help mould who you are and your eventual success. They influence the decisions you make.

> *Always surround yourself with people who are better than you. If you're hanging around bad people, they're going to start bringing you down. But if you surround yourself with good people, they're going to be pulling you up.*
>
> DONNY OSMOND

It's easy to see how people can lose their motivation and desire to go forward. Lose momentum, energy, and the ability to take the right actions. Imagine how hard it is to keep motivated and maintain your energy levels in your own business if you don't have the support of your family and friends. Your core group. Then the ongoing support of your community. You'd be swimming against the current.

Choose for yourself the circles in which you move.

Negative influences

When a business owner doesn't have any support from family or friends (their core), it becomes very difficult to stay motivated within the business for long. Particularly when the family is not being supported financially by the business during difficult times. The core influencers start feeling the pressure and their support wavers. *'Maybe you should go get a job.'* It can feel, to the owner, that ultimate failure is almost a logical destination. The personal community has also gone silent. Because the owner may have slowed down the marketing and communications. Slowly, the negative results will shrink the community. And the upward lift (the wind beneath your wings) turns into a deadly downdraft that can pull the already depressed business owner further into the mire of negativity.

Growth and forward momentum are easier when you move in positive circles of your own choosing.

WARREN RATLIFF

But it's not a given. The business owner can turn it around through mindset. Motivation. Drive. And vision.

We all need support and strength. As kids, we rely on our parents or guardians for that pillar. They offer the strength and support through their very presence (well... usually). Having the support of family, friends, and associates is very important for the owner's mindset.

And when we lose that familial support as a business owner, and your community turns its back on you, the hope upon which you have pinned your goals and aspirations diminishes. If you're continually being asked, 'When are you going to give up and get a job?' the negativity can eventually creep into your mindset. And the business will either fail or you just give up. The strength of the pillar is weakened.

The tribal drum beats just for you

Let's be clear on the difference here between your core surrounding influencers, a coach, a mentor and your personal community – your tribe.

> *A tribe is a group of people connected to one another, connected to a leader, and connected to an idea. For millions of years, human beings have been part of one tribe or another. A group needs only two things to be a tribe: a shared interest and a way to communicate.*
>
> SETH GODIN

Say your car breaks down in the desert:

- Your core influences helped you to choose the car and waved you off on your trip
- Your mentor will share his wisdom of when that very same thing happened to him (or her) and how they took care of it
- Your tribe (community) will be in behind, pushing the car to the nearest help

- Your coach will ask you the right questions that will allow you to work out your options to finish the trip under your own steam - and learn from the experience

From that analogy, you can (hopefully) gather that your tribe might include your coach and / or your mentor. They form a part of it - not standing to one side watching.

The influences of tribes

Imagine you've washed up on a desert island. The only other people on the island are pirates and thieves (and maybe a volleyball named Wilson). These are your new community. After three weeks of living, eating, being with this new community, what characteristics do you think you will have picked up from the group?

If you said that you would be unchanged - then you've probably starved to death as the pirates and thieves took all the bread and water. You would, by natural osmosis, take on their traits - becoming like them to survive. You like bread and water too, right?

Let's say, for the flip side of the same coin, that the island upon which you find yourself is inhabited only by aristocrats and high achievers. Inventors and engineering types. Which way do you think your own character will gravitate? You'd tend towards the thinker. The high achiever. You may have invented a radio beacon from a coconut.

The tribe around you has an amazingly powerful life force that passes on traits to you. And whilst we are all individuals, the collective energy of a positive tribe whose ethics, motivations and visions are shared with you can be a powerful supporting force.

It's the same for small business owners. As important as it is to get support from family, friends and associates, it is also important to look for and mix with other small business owners. Some of whom have already achieved MORE than what you are targeting.

With this being said, your tribe may (and arguably should) include other people who are at or below your current 'level'. People who are starting their own journey.

Within your tribe, you may have people at various milestones – before you, after you and at the end of their own journey, having achieved five times or more what you strive for.

Therefore, it can be helpful to create a tribe of like-minded people who understand where you are and what you're facing. Business owners who have gone through the struggles you are currently facing.

When a business owner doesn't have positive support from their surrounding people and circle, it's hard for them to keep working constructively and pro-actively on the business. Think of a time when you felt down. About anything. Work, health, spirituality, relationships. Did your disappointment creep into other areas of your life? There is a natural bleed of emotion between different areas of your life, and it can be difficult to insulate other areas when you are feeling down in another. How often has a personal problem, a relationship problem, or any other personal issue affected your work life? It's inevitable.

How do you go about creating your tribe?

The simplest and quickest answer here is not to create one, but to join one. The world is old, my friend, and you are not the first to try this. Join the club.

What's the best size and structure of a supportive tribe?

There will be a dynamic to every tribe. And tribes will ordinarily comprise anything from 10 people to a few hundred individuals. Some personalities within the group will want only to say 'Hey' and maybe have a chat. Others might be the continual communicator - emailing and texting at weird hours and odd days. There will always be the 'Sheriffs', watching vigilantly over the behaviours and ethics of the group. There'll be the CEOs (chiefs), worker bees, academics, and dunces.

The mutual thread among them all is the common purpose. The unity with which they take a part in the development and motivation of you. And each other. They are a huge rubber band that flexes and bends but always holds support.

In days gone by: Prior to the enormous number of 'friendships' possible today in social media, there was a popular theory by Robert Dunbar (a British anthropologist and evolutionary psychologist) that humans can maintain no more than 150 relationships at any time. When tribes in past times grew beyond that 150 limit, the theory surmises that a split occurred and the tribe morphed into two potentially competing tribes. How this impacted on a tribe is interesting from the perspective of where exactly the relationships with and within the tribe exist.

Now: The potential to get close to and connect with other like-minded people received a shot of adrenalin with the development and spread of social media. Remember 2004 when Facebook emerged on computers around the globe? No longer limited by geography, topography, meteorology (or any other -ology), you can easily connect with a tribe through the click of a few buttons on your computer screen or smart device. Rather than the past limitation of 150 entities, today you can belong to groups of staggering sizes. Liking, following, commenting, tagging, and hash-tagging have replaced phone calls and personal visits. Some would argue that the lack of personal contact is detrimental to the tribal culture. The benefits that come from an effective tribe are strengthened through personal, as opposed to digital, contact.

Where are your tribe members located? Are they online, in person, in a large group, in a clubhouse, a pub or somewhere else? To be supportive, I believe it's important for a tribe to exist in your version of what's real. Whether online or in person. Or a combination of both. Whether joining a tribe or creating your own, endeavour to create an environment of support.

You should be able to reach out to other members of the tribe individually or collectively when you need support. Or to share a win or a loss.

Either way, find the mentors or coaches with whom you can create a two-way learning relationship. It shouldn't solely be because you need to learn from a bigger and more experienced person. Instead, your goal could be to create a tribe where the mentors or coaches/small business owners are focused on doing the same as you – learning from each other.

Is there a benefit to a smaller tribe?

Firstly, let's define exactly what a small tribe is. There is no real science behind the effectiveness of the size of your tribe. Some people thrive with a tribe of a few, whilst others need thousands in their following to feel fulfilled and empowered. The rise of brand-new businesses such as 'social media influencers' rely on the volume of online followers to create enough power to increase their earning potential. Power by numbers.

Yet most small business owners rely on far more intimate (if you can call online intimate) numbers in their online tribes. They also belong to smaller tribes that still meet in person regularly to support each other and add value. Look at the therapeutic benefits of remedial groups like AA or single parent groups. Sporting clubs and retiree groups are great examples. These groups are extremely effective **because** they meet in person. Should these groups take to the thousands of the online environment, would the tribe be as effective? It is an argumentative point – for discussion over a beer or coffee anytime you want.

For a small business owner, the tribe needs to be carefully selected. Put some thought into where you'll find the most benefit. And the effectiveness of a tribe is often impacted by the business owner's interaction (contribution) with the tribe. Give and you will receive. Then the business owner can similarly offer support to their own team.

If, on the flip side, you don't gather positive support or help from your surrounding circle, you and your business may encounter problems like:

- Lack of productivity and business growth
- Inability to meet the work deadlines
- Messed up work and personal life
- Lack of confidence
- Failure in various business affairs
- Poor health due to improper routine and diet.

Solutions to these problems

We've discussed the most major and obvious problems a business owner can face in their personal and professional life with no surrounding support. Surrounding influences. A positive and like-minded tribe. But what about solving these issues? Of

course, it's impossible to manage everything on your own – in both personal and professional life.

Hence, the best ways to help maintain the support of your tribe is to focus on:

- Keeping your family and friends in the loop with what you're working on. Keep sharing the dream and getting their input on goals
- Being kind to everyone and appreciating their efforts in your life – and letting them know
- Asking them to offer you help in things you can't manage (it's never weak to ask for help yourself)
- Giving some time to your friends and family (at least on weekends) and informing them how their help is important and how important they are to you

Just as you need support, the people around you need appreciation. feedback and kindness to motivate them to keep offering you the support. Think about it from your own personal perspective. What is it that makes you want to help someone? And what feedback or reciprocation would you like to receive afterwards?

The commonality of ideals and purpose will enable a tribe to support every member at different levels.

CHAPTER 6:
GOAL SETTING FOR SUCCESS

A goal is not always meant to be reached; it often serves simply as something to aim at.

BRUCE LEE

High achievers will often tell you to plan what you want to achieve in 10 years, then have a red hot go at achieving the same outcomes within 12 months. There's every chance that you will fail in the overall outcomes. But you will achieve, in those 12 months, far more than you would have had you kept it on a 10-year time frame. Why? Over 10 years, you have time. Plenty of time. Hence, tasks, activity and plans take their place in the queue for your attention. If you think short term for the same outcomes, your focus, motivation, and activity levels will be off the charts. And you will achieve accordingly.

WHAT IS A GOAL?

A goal is an outcome that becomes possible through a series of actions. It is a future or desired result that a person or a group of people imagine, plan and commit to achieve. A goal needs to represent an improvement on the present for it to be valid.

What is the role of goals in a business owner's life? It's easy for any new business owner to figure out setting goals is the most important driving factors for success. There was, after all, some form of goal set when the business was only a thought bubble. A goal was developed that led to the start of the business or its acquisition. And it must have been a goal to start a business that was achieved in the present time, right?

Similarly, every single step or achievement that a business accomplishes could be classified as a milestone towards the business owner's long-term goal. Big goals (I call them BHAGs – Big Hairy Audacious Goals) will often be challenging to achieve, so it's best to break them into a series of smaller goals – milestones. Each milestone will have a timeframe and its achievement (or not) tells the owner whether they are on track to achieve the larger goal.

Setting goals and milestones will help a business owner achieve better outcomes. And keep their vision alive.

How are goals beneficial?

Achieving business success from a stand-still start involves hard work and careful planning. A new business owner may feel overwhelmed and daunted at the prospect of how much there is to do. However, if the owner sets long-term goals, mini goals, milestones, and action plans, that success becomes more tangible.

When you set an outcome for yourself that aligns with your values and beliefs you provide a road map for your sub-conscious mind to follow.

WARREN RATLIFF

To get results, it's beneficial to set a goal in every business (and business development) step. Like steppingstones across a large pond. Every small business owner creates goals, even if they don't realise they are doing it. Small goals around sales, weekly and monthly targets, time with the family, holidays and more. The major challenge here can be the feeling of failure if (when) goals are not achieved.

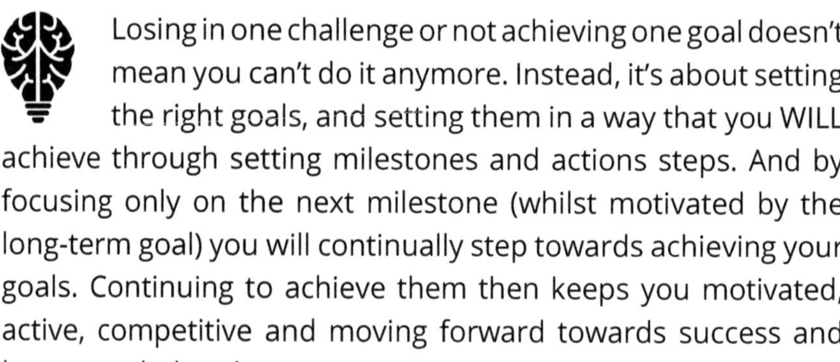

Losing in one challenge or not achieving one goal doesn't mean you can't do it anymore. Instead, it's about setting the right goals, and setting them in a way that you WILL achieve through setting milestones and actions steps. And by focusing only on the next milestone (whilst motivated by the long-term goal) you will continually step towards achieving your goals. Continuing to achieve them then keeps you motivated, active, competitive and moving forward towards success and less overwhelmed.

A business owner's personal goals

When we talk about business owners who have just started a business, they are often striving towards accomplishing multiple life goals. Managing between the professional and personal life can be a struggle. As a result, a businessperson will set multiple goals when starting a new business. And this is crucial to enable the creation of plans and processes.

You wouldn't board a plane if you thought the pilot didn't have a map.

These multiple goals can be in the areas of:

- Personal lifestyle
- Travel
- Hobbies and recreation
- Sports

- Income
- Resources (scale and staffing)
- Health and fitness
- Relationships
- Wealth (often related to income)

While personal goals are important for a business owner (or anyone else), they will often tie in with business goals to keep improving themselves.

For example, 'We'll go on holiday to Hawaii when the business turns over $XXX,' or 'I'll get a new car when we've sold XXX.'

And this style of cross-pollination of ideals and goals is fine. Provided the one that acts as a catalyst (the business success) is realisable through the planning, actions and mindset of the business owner.

Perhaps the second goal, the holiday or the car, could be considered a reward to the business owner for achieving the goal. Rather than being set as a different goal. Which method would motivate you the most?

These personal goals can be for the business owner's personal growth, with the business goals mostly directed towards the business's growth. So there is a difference, yet they can be very closely aligned.

Business goals might also start from a personal goal of starting a business, of building wealth, creating something for the future. The start of the business may be the vehicle that will deliver personal goals, or it may be the goal itself through its very creation.

Setting goals

While having goals may be important, setting the right goals in the right way and giving them their relevant importance is also an important step. Your vision that supports a goal should be sufficiently inspirational and motivating to make you take action towards achieving the goal. Use this same inspiration to see you succeed in whatever area of life you choose - personal or business. The value of the goal needs to be personal.

But how do you give value to your goals? As simple as it sounds, the personal value of goals is, arguably, the main reason we fail in achievement. If you don't see enough value in a goal, it won't happen.

Think for a moment of new year's resolutions. Are these not goals? We've all set them. A few minutes past midnight on the first day of the new year, we make a resolution to do something different, concocted from a dangerous mixture of regret and emotion. What we didn't achieve last year will resurface, with (often) an element of alcohol and peer group pressure. So why are they often forgotten within a week or so? It's because they are unsupported and unstructured goals that are not set in the right way.

When you structure your goals, align your small goals with larger ones with the belief to achieve them. Anything is possible when you have a firm belief that you will accomplish a goal. When you keep on setting milestones towards a specific destination, you will become successful – both in personal and professional life!

Some areas in which a business owner could consider setting goals for their business can include:

- Money
- Activity
- Leadership
- Team
- Relationships
- Wealth
- Health
- Culture
- Passions
- Time and freedom
- Lifestyle
- Customer relationships

The art of setting IMSMART goals

Many people have heard of, and subscribe to, SMART goals. Specific, Measurable, Actionable, Realistic and Tangible. It's a popular format of goal setting that will create a framework around which your goals will have structure and logic.

So why are so many goals, set inside the SMART framework, never fully achieved? There are a couple of elements missing. We've mentioned earlier about passion, inspiration and motivation. By including these in your goals, the nature of the goal takes on new meaning. Having a goal – the achievement of which is a passion – will set up your actions with more clarity and purpose.

Rather than going with the more common structure, a more achievable goal setting structure is the **IMSMART** process:

- **I**nspirational
- **M**otivational
- **S**pecific
- **M**easurable
- **A**chievable (actionable)
- **R**isky (and realistic)
- **T**angible (able to be evidenced).

This IMSMART strategy of setting and accomplishing a goal is derived from some of the most popular concepts for goal setting. The strategy is a combination and inclusive process that includes a heap of empathetic life experience. The simple addition of inspiration and motivation will take the goal to a new level in your ambition to achieve it. Making the goal a little risky adds an element of adventure to it. And the tangibility aspect is how you can show evidence, proof that the goal has been achieved.

I – Inspirational: It needs to INSPIRE you

Setting a goal that inspires you, really digs at your core and fills your thoughts will help start the process. Imagine if your goal did NOT inspire you. Or the goal was set by someone else (maybe your boss) – will it inspire you?

M – Motivating: It needs to MOTIVATE you into action

Your motivation is related closely to what inspires you. The more inspired you are by your goal, the more motivated you will be to take action towards its achievement. A motivating goal will build emotion within you – whether for your business or another area of life.

S – Specific: Being SPECIFIC means dates, numbers

If you set a goal saying, 'I want to better at….' or 'I want to improve at….', maybe, 'Sometime next year I will be….' These are unspecified and don't give you a deadline against which to create milestones and determination. Make your goal specific. Give it a deadline. Use numbers, dates, provable concepts.

M – Measurable: You need to be able to MEASURE progress

Making a goal measurable will allow you to evidence its achievement and progress. Being able to measure your progress, milestones and actions is very important to ensure success.

A – Achievable: Make it ACHIEVABLE yet challenging

Big goals are great. However, if you set goals that are too big, they can create demotivation rather than motivation. Be realistic, yet ambitious with your goals. Go big and make a series of milestones (mini goals) to get there. The 'A' also stands for actionable. Have a goal that enables a clear plan of action.

R – Risky / Realistic / Relevant: RISKY goals keep us on our toes (not dangerous, just risky)

You will probably need to step outside your comfort zone to achieve growth. Making 'safe' goals may not stretch you enough to achieve real growth. You will naturally want to stay in your comfort level. So make it risky. Make it an adventure. And make it realistic (the 'R' stands for both).

T – Tangibility / Accountability: It needs to have TIME and TANGABILITY, so you know when to take steps

This is where you actually provide evidence that you have achieved your goal. The tangibility is the reality factor. Proof. And every milestone needs evidence to prove its achievement. Think of the last thing that needs to happen for you to KNOW that you have achieved your goal.

Whilst not listed here, action is a key part of setting and achieving goals. Your IMSMART goal needs to have a plan. An action strategy that will step you closer with every action you take. You will only achieve your milestones with action because no change is possible without some form of action.

You must take action to achieve a goal. It's logical. And as scary as change can be, as immersed we may be inside our comfort zone, embracing change for the sake of growth is empowering. Strategising your action plan is a great way to remove the fear factor from change.

By following the IMSMART formula and aligning your goals and your values, you, the business owner, can absolutely achieve success.

So, do the math. A new business owner can increase their chances of success by correctly identifying their goals, setting milestones (with timelines) and creating an action plan to get there. Boom!

You might call it a Business Plan.

ACTIVITY 7: Set an IMSMART goal for yourself

Use this template for long-term, midterm and short-term goals.

Take your time on this activity. You might do it once, then come back to it tomorrow or as you think of more that will fit into each box.

Add your GOAL E.g.: By xxx date, I will, I have, I am ...

____

____

____

____

Now fill in the boxes below to put your goal to the test.

I	**Inspirational**	How does it INSPIRE you?
M	**Motivating**	How does it MOTIVATE you into action?

S	**Specific**	Can you make it more SPECIFIC?
M	**Measurable**	How will you MEASURE it?
A	**Achievable**	Is it within grasp?
R	**Risky / Realistic / Relevant**	How is it RELEVANT, a little RISKY and REALISTIC?
T	**Tangible**	Is it TANGIBLE? What's your proof? What's the target date?

Every successful business has a plan – of sorts. Every successful person has an inherent process of goal setting. Every successful person understands success to mean different things. They are all human. And every successful person has endured failures and unaccomplished goals.

Some factors that get in the way include:

- Fear (of change, of fear itself, of failure)
- Procrastination
- Perfectionism (often a cause of procrastination)
- Laziness
- Negativity
- Arrogance
- Negative influences (and influencers)

As long as you know how to set the right goals and attain them, it's easier to avoid business failures and achieve more success in each step.

CHAPTER 7: CAUSE VS EFFECT

WHO'S IN CONTROL OF YOUR BUSINESS AND YOUR LIFE?

The price of greatness is responsibility.

WINSTON CHURCHILL

Have you ever met someone who seems to always be in control? Nothing seems to faze them. They don't get ruffled and, if they do, it's a very short process before they are back to their version of normality. These people tend to attract good things in their life. Attracting success through their actions, whatever success means to them. Not blaming external factors when things go wrong in their own life. Seeming to make things happen for themselves. Always admitting when they are wrong and taking responsibility.

When these people set a goal, they seem to achieve it every time. These people are living at '**CAUSE**'.

Then, on the flip side, other people seem to hover between different levels of negativity. The pessimistic side becomes dominant, and they make decisions from the position of that pessimism. They externalise blame and responsibility for whatever negative things happen. They often find success to be a struggle, hard work. When things don't go exactly to plan, they tend to find a reason why – and it won't be anything they did. It's always someone or something else at fault.

These people are living at **'EFFECT'**.

Cause and Effect.

These are two different aspects of living a life – two perspectives on how we view our lives unfolding. One is the daily drag. The pulling of weeds as we try to harvest success in our life. This is the daily minutia.

The other is the big picture. Ticking items off the bucket list. Creation of your perfect life where, on your 90th birthday, you look back at your timeline with a smile.

Being at Cause or Effect will largely determine how your success will look in the long term.

One day you run late for a meeting.

Do you:

- **A:** Blame the traffic, blame the kids, blame your partner, the weather, your poor sleep patterns, the neighbours, the car – whatever held you up?

Or

- **B:** Take responsibility for your tardiness by accepting and learning from whatever held you up and saying, 'Sorry I'm late, it won't happen again'?

Where did you land? If you were an 'A' – you are on the Effect side of the equation. You are blaming any number of external factors rather than taking responsibility for running late yourself. If you answered 'B', then you are living at Cause. You accept responsibility and learn from the experience.

At Cause	At Effect
Takes responsibility for what happens in their lives	Lays blame on other people, events and things
Takes control of all areas of their life	Allows other people to make decisions on their behalf
Internally driven	Externally driven
Triggers the effects that happen around them	Waits for things to just 'happen' around them

At Cause	At Effect
Create whatever needs to be created for success	Finds excuses for failure or mediocrity
Drives their own bus	Becomes a passenger in their own life
Takes charge of the results that they produce	Finds reasons for not getting the results
Aims for greater achievements and success	Settles on lower achievements and complains about it
Says 'WHY' and 'HOW' to make things happen	Says 'YES' to everything that happens – done by other people
Creates their own version of the future	Satisfied to accept others' successes as their own model
Learns from failure and plans to improve	Gives up when something doesn't work the first time and doesn't learn
Empowered	Dis-empowered

We need to always consider these two sides or aspects when looking at how we live our lives. When we make decisions in personal life or business. Either live with full control of your life and what goes in it (at Cause), or blame others for everything that goes wrong or doesn't happen at all (at Effect).

Have you ever reacted strongly to someone or something, then afterwards, in reflection, thought, 'I could have handled it better'? For example, maybe you've yelled at your kids – for having what they construed not as being naughty but as having fun. Then afterwards, you've regretted how you reacted.

Being at Cause effectively means that a person creates their own circumstances. Through their mindset, positivity and actions. Their own circumstances. Their own environment. Decisions become empowering rather than justifying.

Living at Cause is an empowered stance. Failures become learning experiences – rehearsals for success. It enables positive change and forward momentum. Acceptance of your values and goals and committing to the processes of achieving is a powerful state in which to live. You accept being the cause of everything happening in your life – the good AND the unfortunate. You don't linger in negativity about things that are beyond your control. You adapt. You improvise. You create. And you accept.

Living on the Effect side of the equation is a disempowered position. Stuff happens, and whilst there are many things outside your control, your reaction to the event or situation is what you can control. Taking control of your responses means you are controlling your actions. Your learnings. When you live on the Effect side, you tend not to learn.

Look at the image below. Reasons for poor results are excuses.

BEING AT CAUSE VS BEING AT EFFECT

Creating results ______________________ Finding Excuses

How does this look for a small business owner?

The impact of living at Cause and Effect can profoundly impact a small business. Someone makes a business decision. In small business, it would typically be the owner. Setting their goals for the business and their own life. Being at Cause. Planning and learning. Engaging whatever resources they need to make their goals and ambitions achievable. Taking responsibility.

If the business owner is on the Effect side, then they are blaming external factors for the business not achieving its goals. For example, *'We didn't hit that sales target because the market was quiet / the weather was terrible / the sales rep didn't perform / the government made a bad call.'* Can you see the pattern here?

Acceptance of mediocrity or poor performance is a barometer of the Cause and Effect concept.

Certainly, there are environmental, market and economic factors that will impact a business, and they are beyond any one person's control. Remember, stuff happens. So being at Cause allows the owner to acknowledge these external events, learn from them and quickly act to mitigate any risk created from the event.

A manufacturing business in Sydney's West was producing a unique window treatment application, a liquid formulation, for cars, commercial and domestic windows to make them more water and 'dirt' proof. They were growing rapidly until the COVID-19 pandemic caused shutdowns and revenue losses. The business turnover suffered a significant decrease as the customers stopped spending money and the existing market collapsed. There was a great risk of closedown.

The business learned and improvised. They made a few changes to their processes and started producing hand sanitiser for bulk markets. The business owners were (and still are) at CAUSE and the business has continued strongly as a result.

EXTRACT FROM 15MINUTES4ME.COM

In the right front part of your brain, just above your eyeball, you will find your right prefrontal cortex (PFC). This is the part of the brain which is responsible for your negative thoughts. For people who have thoughts negatively for a long time or experience depression, medical visualization has shown that this part of the brain is hyperactive or overly developed. You could say that it sort of looks like an over-trained muscle in a body builder who uses too many steroids.

Under-developed positive thoughts are developed in your left prefrontal cortex

On the top, left part of your brain, you will find the part which is responsible for your positive and optimistic thoughts. During periods of feeling down, pessimism, stress, or depression, this zone seems to be a bit smaller than the right side. It is under-developed.

Where you place yourself, at Cause or Effect, will positively or negatively impact you, your personal life, your relationships, health, mentality, and your business.

Although the business owner makes the decisions, the reflection and mindset that we spoke about in Chapter 1 link their mindset to what the business can achieve.

It's common (and arguably correct) to view the business and the owner as separate entities. However, there are direct links between the business owner's mindset and the business itself. And the flow on to the lives of staff, family, friends, colleagues - everyone around the owner will be impacted.

A business owner who is living at Cause takes a stance of action and responsibility. They understand that everything in the business holds an element of personal responsibility. So, they empower themselves and the business - as the head of the business. The business culture will benefit from the owner's stance.

If the owner takes the opposite polarity and approaches life and business from the Effect side of the equation, there is a stronger chance of failure. Of acceptance and settling for half achievements. These people are more convinced that whatever happens to them or the business is not their fault. Instead, the things that happen to them are driven by the actions, words, or weaknesses of others. Their vision may be modelled on someone else's, so they aren't motivated to take the Cause stance.

We all, at some point in our life, experience negativity. It's okay to feel sad. To feel angry or demotivated. What's not okay is to stay in those emotions and make decisions from them. Remember, stuff happens. How we deal with negativity or negative emotion will be largely determined by our positioning on the Cause vs Effect scale.

Being a business owner means you need to be in charge of the business you have set up and are running in the present. Making decisions from an informed and a learned position. Steering the ship from the rudder in response to the surrounding seas and not letting the surrounding seas steer you.

Considering this, being on the equation's Cause side can greatly benefit the business owners. They are in complete control of what they do and how they plan. What happens in the business always has a purpose. They take responsibility, rectify (and learn from) their mistakes. As a result, they are better placed to take their business further towards success.

It's different for people living on the Effect side of the equation. Such people are more likely to blame other people or external factors for whatever negativity happens in the business. They don't take responsibility, don't fix or learn from their mistakes. They will struggle to take their business further towards success. Hence, they don't learn and consequently can't improve that issue. They will simply settle.

Do it easy? Or do it anyway?

Simple can be harder than complex: You have to work hard to get your thinking clean to make it simple. But it's worth it in the end because once you get there, you can move mountains.

STEVE JOBS

Where you are positioned on the scale from Cause to Effect comes down to mindset and resources. Our belief patterns. While the Cause side is more beneficial and success-oriented for a business owner in personal and professional life, it's less common than the Effect side.

In fact, the Effect side of the equation is the side that most of the population finds themselves on. Because it's easier. It's staying inside our comfort zone and expecting other people to make changes that will benefit us. As humans, we have a natural aversion to whatever feels more difficult. We like it to be easy.

When you plant a seed, do you commit to watering it or expect nature to do this for you? Who do you blame if the plant dies?

The more difficult pathway is often outside your comfort zone. Taking responsibility and changing your behavioural patterns, whilst the better option, is not easy. Blaming someone else or external factors is simply easier than taking responsibility. Or perhaps you're just scared of change.

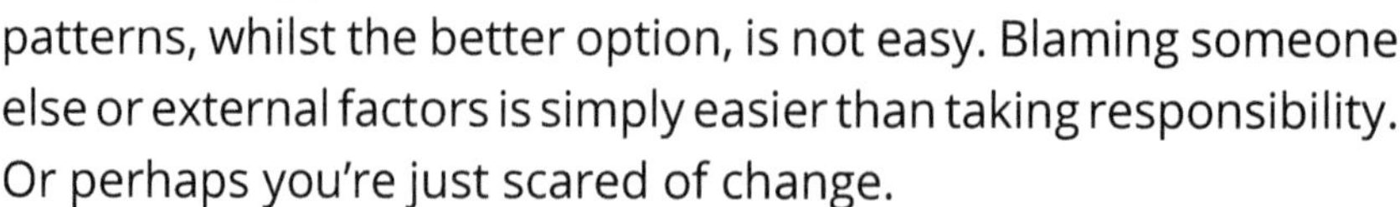

People are very quick to blame something outside of them. Our brain tends to gravitate towards the easier pathway, and the more commonly beaten mental pathway is to become defensive and blame someone or something else. It can be hard work to accept responsibility. To live at Cause. The more common trend is to adopt some negativity in our lives.

Picture life at 95 years old. If you could imagine never having had or created what you truly wanted in your life or your business. It will not be very satisfying, will it? That's if you keep living on the EFFECT side.

How to be in full control and avoid being on the Effect side

We've looked at how being on the Effect side of the equation will probably not help you achieve real success. It's time to understand how you CAN be in control of your life and your business and how to avoid being on the Effect side. When you're a business owner, you need to take the helm, steer the ship, drive the bus. Let others be your passengers because you are a leader. If the business starts to change, the owner needs to step up and lead. Blaming others for the failure and making excuses to your surrounding partners or team and yourself serves very little purpose.

Whether you think of this in your personal life or the professional business world, it's very important to be in control of what you do and how you manage things. In this way, you can avoid playing the blame game. Instead, you'll be the influencer. The controller and the one holding responsibility.

Learn how to be in control, learn from everything that happens, not just selected things that your brain thinks are easier pathways. You'll then be better equipped to realise that even in failure, finding excuses and blaming others is wasting your precious time (a valuable resource for a business owner).

The sense of responsibility and constant learning and achievement will help change the outcome. Your mindset will create a more progress-oriented action plan and the learned decisions will be empowering.

Here are a few ways you can learn to have full control of your life and your business and be on the Cause side of the equation:

- **Create value instead of just serving time:** Your business will require your input and action to achieve success. When making a plan or decision, look at the issue and the desired outcome, and ask yourself what the best value pathway will be. What action can you take that will step you and the business towards your goal? Look at different options and evaluate the value that each option would deliver. Then choose the option of greatest value in terms of time and achieving your goal. If you fail to create options, it can diminish the value of your time through poor decisions. Learn to add value to whatever time you invest in your business; it will be a better and more productive business management strategy.
- **Create a business system that doesn't always need you:** You are the business owner. Think of your life. Your motivation. Create a system within the business that will enable the business to profit without your full-time oversight. In this way, you don't have to always keep that stress level high, and you can also take a break. You can create space in your mind for creative thought, and magic happens in space!
- **Let go and relax when you can:** When we're tired and finding it difficult to keep plugging away, maybe feeling trapped,

that's a time when we are more likely to find excuses and want to stop. Take control at that moment by letting go. Take a short break. Do something that occupies your mind, away from work. Burnout is a real thing and a massive danger for a small business owner. You can still commit to your process whilst honouring your goal and your life. You need to relax to understand how you can control your business further.

- **Get an objective resource:** Many small business owners feel they need to know it all. To control everything, you need to do it yourself, largely because you don't trust anyone else to share the passion with which you approach your own business. An external, objective resource, like a coach or a mentor, will throw a third-party perspective into your business and decisions. The responsibility stays with you, and you will be at Cause. Your perspective will be far broader with someone to bounce ideas off.
- **Always look at the big picture:** Don't forget why you are doing what you are doing. You started the business for a reason. So, to stay on the Cause side, it's important to remember your motivations and goals and remind yourself every day.
- **Get into curiosity mode to want to learn – always:** The empowered person at Cause will always learn from everything that happens around them. School is IN. Accepting new learnings, looking for them, and truly wanting to learn from both positive and negative things will empower you to make decisions from a learned place. When you increase emotion and opt for decision making from an emotional state, you decrease your intelligence in the moment.

- **Surrender to change and create a plan:** When you create a goal and a plan to achieve that goal, it's important to surrender to the process – the plan. Accepting and adopting change is a start. Controlling exactly what change happens, and reacting appropriately to external influences, will see you at Cause.

Once you try implementing these strategies in your business and life, you will see how effectively your life equation changes. Adopt one step at a time – don't push yourself here. Remember, small changes are easier – and your brain will accept 'easier' more rapidly.

Focus on being the driver of your bus. Steer your ship. Your business direction, success and performance can be determined by your ability to control and manage.

Being at Cause will enable control. Control will see you hitting targets. Setting a goal is creating a gap. Your target is to close the gap by achieving the goal. Then, when you close the gap, create a new one by setting another goal, creating continual

CHAPTER 8:
VALUES OF THE BUSINESS OWNER

ARE THEY ALIGNED WITH THE BUSINESS?

It's not hard to make decisions, once you know what your values are.

ROY E. DISNEY

Values are one of the most important aspects of a person's character. They are, essentially, abstract beliefs that serve as guidelines to determine our actions and feelings. We all have them, instilled from our childhood when our core values are defined and developed. Right, wrong, good, honesty, integrity, pride, bad, evil, love, and more. And these values might not change drastically over time at a personal and intimate level, but they are sometimes remodelled through life experiences. As we grow older, we learn to repress some of our core values and publicly display others.

Understanding, identifying, owning, and living by personal values is something that we all do. Our decisions and actions are largely made and done according to the belief systems in our minds. And our belief systems are dominated by our values.

There are two sets of values that we have. External (or golden) values. And internal (or silhouette) values.

The external values are those that we exhibit and boast to other people. When someone asks, 'Who are you?' The answer is usually those values that we feel obligated by society to display: loving, caring, funny, smart, happy, honest, integrity, trustworthy, and more.

There is also a second set of values. Let's call them **silhouette** values. These are those non-publicised internal values that truly drive decisions, actions, and reactions. These are things like being needy, selfish, greedy, narcissistic, wanting, proud, needing to feel loved, and more. Whilst many people will not admit to it, these 'silhouette' values demand attention.

Values are instilled in people through the ages of 0-7 ish. During those years, our subconscious mind accepts what it is told and what we observe in those around us. If you say to a kid of five years old that they are awesome, they'll believe it. If you tell them they are an idiot, they will believe that.

Think of a baby. When it wants something, it has no qualms in letting everyone know. We all know the secret groan if the table or seat next to us is occupied by a small child. When it's unhappy, it gets loud. When the baby is hungry, thirsty, cranky, wet, soiled - whatever - it's the same thing. The baby has an instinctual response to needing something (including some love and attention). Aside from a mother's almost paranormal ability to understand what the baby wants, the cries and screams all tend to sound the same. And the more the baby wants, the louder it gets. So, the baby is pretty needy, huh? Yet we love and nurture babies. We accept they are being instinctive and living by values that, as adults, are frowned upon.

Can you imagine, for a moment, an adult acting as a baby would every time they wanted something?

Over time, and in a society where you are constantly required to ask permission, society forces us to repress our instinctive emotions and silhouette values. As a result, we give in (usually) to the majority rule and develop our external reactions to fulfil our values for the world to see and judge us by.

But guess what? Those needy, selfish, and demanding values don't really leave us just because we repress the reactions to them. Showing politeness does not remove the emotion. We still want something.

Deep inside the skull of every one of us there is something like a brain of a crocodile. Surrounding the R-complex is the limbic system or mammalian brain, which evolved tens of millions of years ago in ancestors who were mammal but not yet primates. It is a major source of our moods and emotions, of our concern and care for the young. And finally, on the outside, living in uneasy truce with the more primitive brains beneath, is the cerebral cortex; civilization is a product of the cerebral cortex.

CARL SAGAN, COSMOS

Similarly, what we are told and taught in our early childhood days stays with us at a subconscious level. Everything we hear, see, understand, and accept in those formative years will always be with us. Maybe buried deep, but still there. Even criminals can see right and wrong. Their life experiences and belief systems have a different code through which they perceive right and wrong, and they act accordingly. You've heard of 'honour among thieves'.

Concepts and perceptions of values and the corresponding decisions and actions they drive develop more prominently in our character as we gain life experience and grow older.

Let's, for a moment, look at those early days when we were mere babes in arms. We were allowed to cry and react to even the smallest things. Needing a hug would turn into a screaming match. And that was okay. All was forgiven as soon as you stopped crying. And you only stopped crying because you received the hug or whatever you really wanted right then. The love was not diminished because you, the baby you, were displaying your silhouette values. When was the last time you heard a baby apologise for farting?

Crying was the only way to communicate what we felt. It was the only way the people around us could understand that something was going on inside that you needed to have addressed. RIGHT NOW.

Now think of how we communicate a similar need as an adult. Is it okay to cry and stomp your feet as an adult whenever you want something? No. There are protocols. Manners. Social behaviour and politeness. Please. Excuse me. Pardon me. Thank you. May I. You may.

Underlying all the pomp and ritual of our highly evolved civility are the real reasons you ask to have those demands met. So what is, at the very core, driving you? What lies beneath your external (golden) values?

Understanding your own 'silhouette' values is what's important. Accept that they are there and OWN them.

Generally, seven silhouette values drive us:

- Attention
- Belonging
- Control
- Superiority

- Sexuality
- Validation
- Money

These values live within all of us. And they truly need to be satisfied. They lie beneath our external (golden) values and drive our decisions. If you are unaware of these or not fulfilling them, you will feel less satisfied and negative emotions may bubble to the surface (anger, sadness, fear, hurt, guilt).

Say you were having a rough time at work. The boss(es) never seemed to notice you. You felt unappreciated. You were wondering about your future. So you went to visit your mother. Why does that make you feel better? What value is being satiated through the maternal visit? Notwithstanding the familial love you have for your mum (and vice versa) perhaps you are responding to your silhouette value of belonging or validation. Or needing attention.

There are several ways to explore your true values and to understand your silhouette values. Identifying your personal values is an important step to creating the life that will see you fulfilled. And your values will change over time and life experience. Once you find a process that works to uncover your silhouette values, repeat it every six months to see how things change. The following exercise may help.

ACTIVITY 8: Silhouette values identifier

Use this activity to drill into the true feelings you have around certain activities and decisions. Understanding what truly drives you, your silhouette values, helps you align your goals and values.

Today's date: ______________________________

1. What goal would you like to focus on?

____

____

____

2. What can you do NOW that will step you toward that goal (a WANTED NEW Action)? (This will be called '**A**'.)

____

____

____

3. What are you doing INSTEAD of that new action – what current action is preventing you from doing it? (This will be called '**B**'.)

____

____

____

4. Complete the sentence: I really want to do (**A**) but I find that (**B**) gets in the way and stops me.
   Example: I really want to get my golf handicap below 10, but doing my lawns stops me playing golf – it gets in the way.

   - E.g.: I really want to create my marketing but going to work is in the way.
   - E.g.: I really want to do some coaching but spending time with my family is in the way.

I really want to (**A**)________________________________but (**B**)

____

I really want to (**A**)________________________________but (**B**)

____

I really want to (**A**)________________________________but (**B**)

____

5. What are the true (and selfish) feelings that you get when you do (**B**) (What value in you is being satisfied at the deepest level?)

____

____

____

6. What unspoken (gratifying, selfish, guilty, self-indulgent) feeling in you is being satisfied when you do the current action (**B**)? *(Dig deep here)*

____

____

____

7. If you were the most self indulgent, egotistical person on earth what would you get out of the current action (**B**)? (This will be your Hidden Silhouette Value(s)

____

____

____

Can values conflict affect your business?

There are different forms and shades of values. We've been looking at golden values and silhouette values. The outward and the inward. What you will readily fess up to a stranger as opposed to what you would tell your closest, longest friend.

For a business owner, there's no difference. Just because you own a business doesn't mean you are exempt from the need to satiate your silhouette values. It just means that you may feel a greater need to show only the golden values and push the silhouette values even deeper in front of staff, clients, suppliers, and stakeholders. Hide the fact that you need to feel liked by staff. Ignore that feeling to put up the professional front. This is a volcano building pressure. It creates conflict – internally.

It's often the conflict of values rather than the values themselves that can impact the business owner's behaviour and decisions. For example, when a business owner has to discipline a staff member, and they've always loved peace and harmony (avoided confrontation), the situation creates a conflict that will see neither of these values fulfilled.

Whilst it's important to look at the satisfaction of and guidance from our values, it's also important to look into potential conflicts of values. It's this conflict that can lead to procrastination, self-doubt, insecurity, and more.

A recent client in the wholesale trade in Sydney wanted to increase the business and generate a better lifestyle for himself and his family. He knew the additional work involved with the client acquisition would mean more hours at the office. He was okay with that. Until it kept him from bath time with his four-year-old son. He wanted more clients – but he also wanted more time with his family. There were conflicting values around family and work that created a block. The family time won. We've since created scaling and outsourcing so that he can achieve both, but the conflict stopped his business growth for ten years!

Business owners have a personal and professional life, right? Their personal life may include a home, family, circle of friends. The core values were implanted through the value years (remember – 0-7 ish). Then there is the business life. Whilst the two (or more) worlds exist in parallel, the owner's values are split across multiple areas of life. Notwithstanding the very real concept of 'professionalism', it's sometimes very difficult to flick an internal switch to (re)act a certain way to whatever is happening around you, depending on where you are mentally at that moment.

Belief systems, history, education, culture, age, experience all play a part in how anyone reacts to an action or event according to (among others):

- Individual values
- Family values (which is often stated AS a value)
- Team-based and cultural values
- Spiritual values
- Relational values
- Organisational values
- Societal values
- Business values

Let's dig a little deeper.

How do these conflicts show up in the business?

When you created or bought your business, you had a map of who and what the business would represent in your mind (and hopefully in a business plan). What clients would say about you and the business once they've been exposed to both in some way.

Our personal values are who we are. The business values are who the business is. Can you see where I'm going here? Are you pickin' up what I'm puttin' down?

If the personal values of a business owner create a conflict issue for him or her to take money from people, there is a massive conflict of values that will thwart business revenues. For example, *I want to sell stuff but I don't like asking for money.* Can you see the potential problem here? And this concept is particularly strong in service-based businesses. Where you need to apply a value to your time and service, then be willing to back that stance in front of potential clients.

Here are a couple of examples from my experience:

I'm a coach. I know many coaches who enter the industry and start a coaching business for all the right reasons (like there could be a wrong one). They want everything to be warm and fuzzy for their clients and everything just swims along. The main focus is to attract their first potential client after giving them a series of calls and meetings to help them. They delivered a lot of help for free. Then they look at their bank statement and realise that they're not making money by giving it away all the time. Now they feel confronted and awkward on the next call to the client trying to sell them into a paid program. And the client senses this and backs away.

The conflict of values here between the coach and the business stopped a paying client from coming onboard.

A recent client (a franchisee) had been in the business for over five years and had a lot of great experience in the industry. In his franchise were over 15 postcodes where he had rights to sell his products. He hated selling because he didn't like the intrusion and rejection. He had a phobia about contacting someone and asking for their business. Yet the business model was to sell across all the postcodes. After five years, his business revenue came from one (yes, one) postcode only. His activity levels dropped away until he simply waited for the phone to ring or a customer to walk in the door. He filled his time on YouTube.

We have since created scripting for cold reach-out calls to offer help, not sell, and his turnover is now increasing from his other postcodes.

His personal values of needing to be wanted, feeling appreciated and wanting to be respected stopped the business from growing, as he wouldn't risk the rejection of a cold call.

A small business owner needs to shift things around to ensure there are no conflicts in the alignment of values between life and business. Then understanding the concept of values conflict in themselves AND their staff will enable the business AND the owner to move forward AND feel fulfilled.

> *The negative effects of **workplace values conflict** can include work disruptions, procrastination, decreased productivity, project failure, absenteeism, loss of turnover and valued staff termination. Emotional stress can be both a cause and an effect of workplace values conflict.*

In an effective business, your team members also take part in running the business at a strategic level. Their values and personal beliefs will affect your decisions as the owner. The commonality of goals, shared values and alignment will create a harmonious workplace where growth and success are the result.

How do you own and align your values?

A great and proven pathway to becoming that successful business owner that was a part of your original plan is to confidently OWN and RESPECT the values that define you. Then, you can replicate the exercise to identify your silhouette values to get them all out and on paper.

But here's the rub ... they change.

Over time, more experience, failures, wins, trauma, life, and our values morph as we grow older. This is not a set-and-forget type process. Instead, it's an ongoing self-development process to come to grips with WHY you do what you do and how you feel at any given time – subject to your changing environment.

It's largely a process of accepting who you are at an honest, vulnerable, and self-reflective level. And the satisfaction of which values drive you at specific times.

For instance:

- If you want abundance, then realise that you want abundance in your life – accept it and own it.
- If you need to be wanted, or loved, or respected – accept it and own it.
- If you are in business and DON'T have money as one of your top values – think about rechecking your values. It's important to make money, right?
- If you feel you need to be respected – own it (and earn it).

Once you accept these values, then decision making becomes easier.

A small business owner who understands this will also recognise specific traits in other people. Yes, some hide their true feelings very well. But adopting a non-judgmental approach to others will help the small business owner understand his team, clients, and (most importantly) themselves.

Aligning values with goals will then seem a natural thing to do. This alignment is critical for small business owners, for themselves AND their businesses.

Alignment – say a small business owner loves what they do. Every day is a dream for them to go to work. Their goals include retiring in five years and living in a resort somewhere fabulous, with a residual income from the business to enable a lifestyle of abundance. They work hard to grow the business, which relies on them being there all the time – which is no chore, as they love it!

Can you see the flaw? If the business NEEDS the owner to be there at all times, and the owner wants to get away by creating a residual income stream, there is a conflict. Unless rectified in either the goals or the business operations, the conflict will prevent success. And realigning the owner's and the business's values will help in the achievement.

Self-assessment

By self-assessing your values, your team's values, and your business values, you can better understand what matters the most to you and your business. You and your team can also evaluate what matters the most to them.

After this self-assessment process, another huge benefit that you as the business owner can achieve is understanding if your team's values align with your organisational values. If they don't, you know why the values are causing you unsuccessful outcomes in the business.

Besides, at the end of the day, what you and your business team's values need to do is help a business succeed. Suppose the values collide in between the success of your organisation. In that case, you need to find potential solutions to shape your team member's values or go for replacements to make sure that your business values aren't compromised in any way!

With self-assessment, a business owner can allow the business to run according to the owner's values for the business. And identifying and documenting the values is important. Get the message out to the people who need to understand the business values. Getting everyone in the business to live by and apply those values is another challenge for the owner. The owner and their executive leadership team (if they have one) need to lead by example. And they need to understand how the values of their staff align with the business objectives. In this way, a business can achieve higher success standards following the business owner and team values.

ACTIVITY 9: Identify your top 10 values

Values Step 1 – Brainstorming

This brainstorming exercise is for you to learn about the REAL you – so allow about 30 minutes to start with:

- Aim for a list of 30-50 things that answer the question: 'What's most important to me in my life at the moment?'
- Write them down then leave it. Revisit your list after a day or so and write down anything else that comes to mind
- Don't dwell on your responses. Just use whatever words or phrases spring to mind'
- Use the list of examples on the following page if you struggle to think of anything. And just pick the ones that resonate with you in the moment at any level. Don't overthink it.
- And don't judge your answers – or 'cherry-pick' values you think you should have
- If it helps, consider sometimes when you've felt angry or upset, and what was going on that caused that reaction
- Think about times when you have been really happy or enjoying yourself and what caused that

Abundant
Accepted
Accepting
Accomplished
Accountability
Achievement
Adaptable
Admiration
Adventure
Affectionate
Ambitious
Appreciated
Attractive
Approval
Beautiful
Calm
Comfortable
Committed
Communicate
Community
Compassionate
Competent
Concerned
Confident
Conflicted
Connected
Contented
Contributor
Courageous
Creativity
Curious
Decisive
Eager
Easy going
Encouraged
Enthusiastic
Ethical
Exciting
Exuberant
Fairness
Faithful
Flexible
Feminine
Flirtatious
Focused
Forgiving
Freedom
Friendly
Fun
Gay
Generous
Genuine
Giddy
Giving
Goal Oriented
Grateful
Gratefulness
Gratification
Gratified
Growing
Happy
Helpful
Honest
Hopeful
Humorous
In control
Independent
Informed
Innovative
Integrity
Intimacy
Intimate
Involved
Joy
Kind
Leader
Learning
Lovable
Loving
Loyal
Magnificent
Manipulator
Masculine
Mentoring
Optimistic
Organised
Passionate
Peace of mind
Peaceful
Pleased
Pleasure
Positive
Powerful
Praise
Productive
Proud of self
Quite
Religious
Results
Oriented
Rewarded
Risk Taking
Romantic
Satisfaction
Security
Sense of
humour
Sensitive
Serenity
Sharing
Sincere
Soft
Spiritual
Spontaneous
Strategic
Successful
Support
Tender
Thoughtful
Tolerant
Traditional
Trusted
Trusting
Trustworthy
Unconditional
Understanding
Winner
Wisdom
Youthful

WHAT'S MOST IMPORTANT TO ME IN LIFE

1. ______________________________

2. ______________________________

3. ______________________________

4. ______________________________

5. ______________________________

6. ______________________________

7. ______________________________

8. ______________________________

9. ______________________________

10. ______________________________

11. ______________________________

12. ______________________________

13. ______________________________

14. ______________________________

15. ______________________________

16. ______________________________

17. ______________________________

18. ______________________________

19. ______________________________

20. ______________________________

21. ______________________________

22. ______________________________

23. ______________________________

24. ______________________________

25. ______________________________

26. ______________________________

27. ______________________________

28. ______________________________

29. ______________________________

30. ______________________________

31. ______________________________

32. ______________________________

33. ______________________________

34. ______________________________

35. ______________________________

36. ______________________________

37. ______________________________

38. ______________________________

39. ______________________________

40. ______________________________

41. ______________________________

42. ______________________________

43. ______________________________

44. ______________________________

45. ______________________________

46. ______________________________

47. ______________________________

48. ______________________________

49. ______________________________

50. ______________________________

Values Step 2 – Brainstorming (wrap-up)

To wrap up your brainstorming, AT LEAST one week after completing the table in Step 1, complete these final actions:

- Review your brainstormed list from Step 1 and add any new items that have come up since you completed the list
- Now refine it (this is the first refinement)
- Anything you can DO or HAVE may not a value. Look over your brainstormed items and if it is something you can do or have, ask yourself, 'What does that give me?' then keep asking yourself until you get to the value underneath. For example, Travel could be Adventure or Learning, Colour

could be Beauty and Food could be Fun or Community. Cross out the old word and write your new value word in the same spot.

Values Step 3 – Review and condense

Next, we want to review and condense the list of values, feelings, ideas and words you've come up with so far to 10 key factors or values that you will work with going forwards.

- Look for and group similar items together
- Pick the most meaningful word from each group to place at the front and place all the similar items after the most meaningful word, separating each item with '/' and list them in the table below

For example, if Integrity was your most meaningful word, then Honesty, Trust and Truth might all fit alongside like this: Integrity/Honesty/Trust/Truth.

Again, don't overthink it. This is from YOUR mind and is subject to any judgement. It doesn't matter if it's not 100% correct – group them according to what makes sense to you.

NOTE: Don't worry about putting your Top 10 items in priority order – we do the prioritisation in Step 4.

MY TOP 10 VALUES

1.____

2.____

3.____

4.____

5.____

6.____

7.____

8.____

9.____

10. _______________________________________

Values Step 4 – Prioritisation

This prioritisation process takes a bit of thought. This is where you get to see what's REALLY important to you. You may well be surprised by your final value priorities – and if so, that's great, because now you'll have a new, more meaningful way of looking at your life. Follow these steps:

Using just the first word from your Top 10 list items (groups) in Step 3, roughly prioritise your list in the left-hand column below (QUICKLY – this is a 1-minute job!)

Take the first value (A) on your list below and compare it to the second item (B). Do this by answering the following question:

"If I had to choose between having (A) and NOT (B), OR having (B) and NOT (A) for the rest of my life – which would it be?"

If (A) wins (it resonates or means more to you in the moment), then compare (A) to the next item (C) on your list. Use the same question, 'Would I rather have (A) and NOT (C), or (C) and NOT (A) for the rest of my life?'

Keep working your way down the list until an item beats A .... If you get to the bottom of your list and nothing beats (A), then (A) is your top value. Write (A) in the number 1 spot in the right-hand column and start the process again with (B)

If an item beats (A), for example (E), simply continue the question process down the list using the new 'most important' value of (E). Continue from where (A) got to – if (A) beat all the items above, then (E) will too!- If you get to the bottom of the list and nothing beats (E), then (E) is your top value. Write (E) in the number 1 spot in the right-hand column- Return to (A) and repeat the process down the list from (F) onwards to see if anything else beats (A)- If (A) now beats all remaining values, it is your second most important value. Place it in the number 2 spot in the right column

Repeat this process until you have a prioritised order for your values

MY INITIAL TOP 10 VALUES (NOT IN ORDER)

1.____

2.____

3.____

4.____

5.____

6.____

7.____

8.____

9.____

10. _______________________________________

MY FINAL TOP 10 VALUES (IN ORDER)

1.____________________

2.____________________

3.____________________

4.____________________

5.____________________

6.____________________

7.____________________

8.____________________

9.____________________

10. ____________________

You can do this exercise with friends, family or staff to align your values, the business values and your staff values.

Understanding the importance of values, the concept of silhouette values and then aligning all the right people on the same page is an important piece of the business success puzzle.

Remember that your values change over time – just as you do!

Values will change over time and circumstance. Do this exercise every six months to get a grip on what values of yours need to be addressed and what you can do to truly align yourself with your changing values. Return to this chapter every six months. Redo or simply review your values.

Especially if you're looking for ideas or are feeling bored, tired, fed up, or frustrated in your life.

CHAPTER 9: STRESS AND ANXIETY

EMOTIONAL OVERFLOW

Worry a little bit every day and in a lifetime you will lose a couple of years. If something is wrong, fix it if you can. But train yourself not to worry. Worry never fixes anything.

MARY HEMINGWAY

Have you ever tried bending a piece of metal to find that it will bend so far, turn a pale shade... then break? Or try bending a piece of wood to find that cracks appear in the wood at a certain point as you apply force, and if you keep applying pressure, it breaks?

Both the metal and the wood, and any other item that you choose to bend beyond its design, have tolerances beyond which there will be damage to the structure and integrity of what you are bending. By bending it, we are causing stress on the item. When it bends to the point where it becomes damaged. it's reached its stress tolerance level.

The word 'stress' is used in physics to refer to the interaction between a force and the resistance to counter that force. Everything has a tolerance level. Everything at some point experiences stress.

Think of a storm. Mother nature's fury can unleash incredible forces that apply pressure to whatever lies in its path. Trees will bend. Drains and gutters will fill and overflow. Rivers and lakes will flood. They all reach that tolerance level beyond which is overflow or damage. The tree uproots if pushed too far. The drains will overflow.

Stress is actually all around us. All the time. Engineers make a living from understanding the physical nature of stress on buildings, roads, bridges and more. Stress is a physical thing.

Now put that into the context of business and look at where stress can make an impact. The business owner takes on the mantle of responsibility for not only the business but also, to a degree, all stakeholders – staff, family, customers and anyone else who is associated with the business. Understanding this concept is important for everyone. How often have you heard of poor performance or bad behaviour justified (or at least explained) because the person is 'under a lot of pressure'?

As humans, notwithstanding the whole 'opposable thumbs thing', we are separated from most of the animal kingdom because we are blessed with emotions and feelings, the ability to reason (argue) and communicate. And stress can appear within us in a number of ways. I'm not saying that other animals don't feel stress. They do. But we tend to dwell on it and let it run our lives a little more than the rest.

There's the obvious physical stress. If a tree falls on you, there's a fair chance you will suffer damage. If you hit your hand with a hammer, you may break a bone. If you exercise too hard, you will feel the tell-tale soreness in your muscles. That would be physical stress. And that can lead to emotional stress – after you've been injured by a falling tree or the workout blues.

Stress is the state of emotional, physical and / or mental strain or tension that results from perceived or real adverse circumstances and events. Stress is your body's response to anything that requires attention or action.

For the sake of simplicity (yes, I'm a believer in keeping things simple) in this chapter, we'll be looking at emotional and mental stress and its effects on us as humans.

So, what is stress?

Generally, most people use the word stress to refer to negative experiences that leave us feeling overwhelmed. 'I'm stressed out', or 'They are a stress head' being relatively common terms and indicating a negative state in either yourself or another person.

But thinking about stress exclusively as something negative doesn't really define the true nature of stress. Thinking a little more scientifically, stress is a reaction to a changing and demanding environment. It's really more about our own capacity to handle change than it is about whether that change makes us feel good or bad. Change happens all the time, and stress is, for the most part, what we feel when we are reacting to it.

We've discussed the necessity and unavoidability of change. We've also discussed procrastination, activity, goal setting and the cause-and-effect concept. All these concepts are steering you toward accepting change. Because stress is a potential consequence if you don't.

As the metal bar and the piece of wood broke when their tolerance was met, you also have your breaking point. Your business, you within the business, your staff and friends are the same. Think back to when a significant change was made, at either a personal level or in your business, that impacted your daily routine. Think of a time when you had to make a decision to change something – a process, a system, a price –

because you needed to react to a potentially negative situation. The recent pandemic and the forced changes to business (and hence business owners) are a good example. The stress levels on business were enormous as we were restricted from seeing family and friends and many businesses were forced to close. Some more than once. The metal bar of business stress tolerance was bent because of a very stressful situation, and everyone reacted differently.

What happened in your business? Where did stress materialise, and what were the consequences? By adapting, surviving, changing, and morphing your daily routine and the business towards the new normal, you were managing stress. Think about how you adapted with your business and managed the stress to go with it. Whatever your outcome, if you're reading this book, it means that you survived at some level. Now is the time to re-evaluate and plan the future.

Without planning, flexibility, and acceptance (demanding) of change, you can feel overwhelmed, and that can lead to stress.

There is a lot of information online and thorough research about stress and I would encourage you to look deeper into it (without getting stressed about it) to find out more details if you wish. There are whole volumes written about stress and its effects. It's dangers. Again, for simplicity, we'll be taking the 'view from the plane' version in this chapter, relating stress to small business and, specifically, its owners.

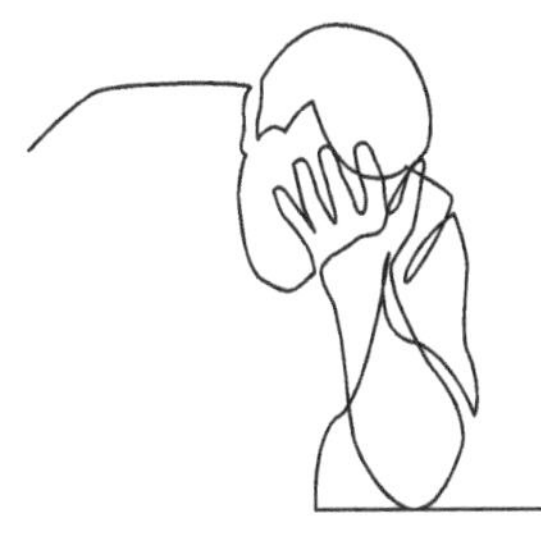

Anxiety – is that a form of stress?

Have you ever noticed how some people tend to react strongly when, say, it gets windy or stormy? They start worrying about what might happen. Remember the falling tree? People suffering with anxiety will worry about the tree before it falls. Will the wind do any damage? Will the storm create a flood in the home? There are thousands of possibilities, yet they worry about what they fear might happen. As soon as the storm clouds gather, they might start to worry about the damage that may happen IF the storm hits and IF it's a bad one.

There are many areas in business where owners typically feel the storm fear. Sales levels are a very common one. 'What if the sales don't improve?' 'What if my margins are squeezed, and the profit drops away?'

> ***Anxiety** is generally the sense of fear, unease, worry or nervousness about something in the future – that has not happened as yet. It is a sense of anticipated failure, danger, trouble or threat.*

Business owners, as we've discussed already, make decisions many times every day. And anxiety is common in many of those decisions, particularly strategic and important ones that will affect other people. Add to that the scenario where a business owner has no tangible support. No one to talk to where ideas and options can be bounced around. The decision is producing anxiety. There's a feeling of foreboding that can creep into the mindset of the business owner, and it often means that the decision is made defensively or put off for another time. Remember Chapter 3 on procrastination?

That feeling is often driven by what has happened to them in the past, and the beliefs that they have formed around that past event – then applied to things that have not happened yet. The future.

For example, they may have been through a bad storm some years ago where they were injured or frightened. Perhaps someone close to them was hurt. From that time onward, they have felt anxiety about storms. It's an internally induced reaction based on past events, but the worry is over future storms. Their belief system created a fear that bad things happen in storms.

Another great example is where a student is feeling anxiety about an upcoming exam. It hasn't happened yet, hence the internal trigger to a future event can cause symptoms.

There's a thin line between stress and anxiety, sometimes very thin. Both are emotional responses, and both can have similar effects on us. But where anxiety is an internal response over a future event, stress is typically caused by an external trigger – something that has already happened or is happening.

The trigger that brings on the feeling can be short term, such as a work deadline or a fight with a loved one. Or long term, such as being unable to work, discrimination, or illness – chronic or otherwise.

What are the symptoms? How do I recognise stress?

One of the tricky things about stress is that it can manifest itself in a wide range of physical, physiological, mental, and emotional symptoms in people.

Indeed, stress symptoms can affect your body, your thoughts and feelings, and your behaviour. And there are short-term symptoms that can, if left unchecked, result in long-term problems.

So being able to recognise common stress symptoms can help you manage them. Of course, knowing your own body and mind helps, so that irregularities can be identified. If, for example, in your business there is a function that involves loud noise (maybe machinery or plant operation), then getting headaches may be commonplace. Hence, a headache as a symptom of stress may be unnoticeable in that situation.

Stress that's left unchecked is known to contribute to many long-term and chronic health problems, such as high blood pressure, heart disease, obesity, and diabetes.

People under stress may experience mental and physical symptoms. As a rule of thumb, here are a few commonly known symptoms of stress.

Physical effect	Mood and attitude	Behavioural
Headache	Anxiety	Eating disorders
Muscle pain and tension	Restlessness	Anger

Physical effect	Mood and attitude	Behavioural
Chest pain	Lack of focus	Drug or alcohol use
Fatigue	Lack of motivation	Smoking
Libido (sex drive)	Feeling overwhelmed	Withdrawal (social)
Mouth ulcers and soft tissue soreness	Irritability	Inappropriate laughing
Digestive problems	Insecure	Sleep disorder

Anxiety leads to a nearly identical set of symptoms: insomnia, difficulty concentrating, fatigue, muscle tension, and irritability.

In a small business environment, the effects of stress and anxiety on the owner will impact directly on the business. The business may be the cause of the stress, and often is. There can be a cycle – a 'Catch 22' if you like, where the business causes stress and then the owner suffers, triggering poor performance (for themselves AND the business), which causes more stress. Then the stress, like a contagion, spreads to staff and stakeholders. A cycle begins and expands unless the causes of the stress are addressed.

The potential consequences on the owner, his or her community, and core influencers can be disastrous.

What can stress and anxiety do to you and your business?

Stress impacts our lives at multiple levels. There are the obvious personal health implications, the short-term symptomatic ones potentially leading to debilitating long-term and chronic health problems. It can impact your behaviour, which can then impact performance at work, in sport, in relationships and more. You may have heard the term 'worry yourself into an early grave'?

For a business owner, the implications here reach beyond the personal. The business itself can be under stress because the owner is feeling it. Then there are the staff, stakeholders, family and friends who can feel the effects of stress. The flow-on effect of a stressed owner can have huge impacts throughout the business.

Let's say an owner is under financial stress because the business is not really making the money that they planned. Sales are soft, for whatever reason. It seems like nothing the owner does makes a difference. The mounting stress on the owner changes their behaviour. Desperation can creep into the sales skills, as they really need to convert every lead and make every sale. And that pressure affects the customers' willingness to buy.

In product sales environments, the owner becomes reticent to buy stock because of the outward cash flow. Stock shortages affect the buyers, so they shop somewhere else. The owner puts more pressure on sales staff to make sales at higher margins. The salesperson then feels stress mounting to protect their job, and the cycle spirals.

Let's say the owners' stress is coming from a personal issue. Relationship issues are a very common cause of stress and the knock-on effect of the stress flows from personal life into the business. A 'why bother' attitude will be noticed by staff, customers, and maybe even suppliers. When the owner is depressed or at low energy levels because of stress or anxiety, this can bring into the workplace a negative contagion that can cripple a business.

Behavioural indicators of stress can include:

- Withdrawal from other people, including staff, customers, friends, family, colleagues, and associates, or you may find yourself snapping at them. Losing patience is a potential sign of stress
- Becoming indecisive or inflexible – this can affect decision making and efficiency within the business and potentially stagnate any business growth
- Suffering exaggerated emotions – becoming tearful or covering up with misplaced humour in front of other people in the business
- Problems getting to sleep or staying asleep – the 3am think tank may have you staring at the ceiling most nights
- Experiencing sexual problems (maybe not too much of it....) with performance and reduced sex drive
- Indulging in vices such as smoke, alcohol or drugs more than usual. The pub visit after work becomes a more commonplace event

Physically your body might suffer from:

- Headaches
- Nausea
- Indigestion
- Shallowness of breath or hyperventilation
- Excessive sweating – including night sweats

- Heart palpitations or some form of arrhythmia
- Joint and muscle aches and pains

Long-term implications are far and wide and might rely on underlying medical conditions that are already prevalent in you.

But a few typical long-term consequences can include:

- If the stress is long term, you may notice your sleep patterns diminish and your memory may be affected
- Your eating habits change – grabbing meals at odd times or suffering from eating disorders
- Lethargy and feeling less inclined to exercise

While the symptoms of stress we've discussed here are related to you personally, they can have a direct, and indirect, impact on your business and those around you.

Your doctor needs to be consulted if you feel you are suffering any symptoms that cannot be explained as 'normal'. Stress can be a silent killer, so treat it as such and consult medical advice for yourself.

The symptoms and effects of stress that are listed in this book are typical and common. But all symptoms are subjective to you, as an individual, and under no circumstances should this book be used as a reference to self-diagnose nor treat any medical condition.

How can you help yourself deal with stress and anxiety?

Here are some things you can do daily to help control stress in your personal life and as a business owner.

1. Understand yourself, your mind and body so that you can recognise when you are feeling stress.

Understanding yourself and knowing your own physiology, mind responses and health will place you in a stronger position to quickly recognise common symptoms of stress. Take into consideration what potentially stressful situations are presenting, or about to present (for anxiety), and try to connect the physical and emotional signals that you're experiencing to whatever pressures you are facing. Don't ignore physical warning signs such as tension, moodiness, irritability, muscle aches, tiredness, or headaches.

When you feel stressed, think about its cause. Write the causes down and make a few notes about each item on the list, then sort them into categories:

- Controllable issues with a simple practical solution
- Controllable things that will improve over time if they don't escalate
- Things that are outside your control

If you have no control over something, there is no point worrying about it, nor being anxious over a future event. Be flexible and prepared to fix whatever is wrong through decisive and forward moving action. Take small steps if it is a large problem. Plan your strategy to deal with it, write down the strategy, and create your action plan.

Taking small steps towards the things you can improve will give you control. If you feel overwhelmed, ask for help. It's also ok to say no to things you can't take on.

2. Look at your schedule and task list

What are you attempting but not completing? Are you taking on too much? A common business strategy, particularly for small business owners who feel that they are the only ones who can do what needs to be done, is to automate or delegate.

Could you hand over some things to someone else? If there is something that needs to be done, and you are too busy or not skilled to do it, shift it. Perhaps you could extend the timeframe in which you are trying to achieve tasks. Can you do things in a more leisurely way? You may need to change your list of priorities and reorganise your work, your business or your life so you're not trying to do everything at once.

3. Look to your team and your tribe. Build supportive relationships

Re-read Chapter 5 and look deep at your team, your core influencers and your personal community. Find people who may be able to take some of the emotional burden from your shoulders. Sometimes just having someone that you can really talk to, at a vulnerable and trusting level, will help release stress.

Think of joining a club or doing a training course to expand your interests and increase your social network. Do something different. There are usually plenty of organisations looking for volunteers and that will help change your perspective and have a beneficial impact on your mood.

4. Eat healthily

We are what we eat. And in times of stress, we might find ourselves either comfort eating the wrong foods, or not eating much at all. Eating disorders are a real disease and medical advice should be sought if you cannot break this cycle.

You can improve your mood and your mental wellbeing with a healthy diet when you include enough nutrients (including essential vitamins and minerals) and water.

5. Keep a sense of humour

We all have a sense of humour. It's part of being human. What varies is the stimulus for triggering our humour. So whatever tickles your funny bone, do more of it. Go see a live comedian. Watch some of your favourite comedy shows, or a funny movie.

Whilst it's clichéd to the max, be prepared and ready to laugh at yourself. Short of some masochistic self-deprecating talk, have a laugh at something you did that was funny.

6. Be aware of your smoking and drinking (and other vices)

We all have vices. And at the risk of another cliché, moderation is the key. If you suddenly realise that you are smoking more or drinking more than you normally would, then be prepared to face it and work out what silhouette value you're trying to satisfy through that vice.

Whilst drinking may provide a short-term buzz where problems become inconsequential, it can make problems worse. Alcohol and caffeine can increase feelings of anxiety.

7. Get regular physical activity and exercise

I know, I know, here's the old chestnut... exercise. Healthy mind, healthy body. But it's true!

Mindset is closely related to physiology. Physical exercise produces endorphins that boost your mood and can help manage the effects of stress. You may have heard of people getting in the zone when they exercise. Even a little physical activity can make a difference, such as walking for 15-20 minutes three times a week or whenever you can.

8. Take time out to recharge

It may be a weekend now and then, or a week here and there, but getting away to recharge is a really important part of managing stress. Think of a V8 supercar. As fast as they go, and for as long as they race, they all take pit stops and change drivers regularly.

Make a point and put in your calendar some 'me-time' every week. Every three months, take a recharge break and leave the phone at home. Take time to relax and practise self-care, where you do positive things for yourself, like doing a hobby or sport. Make time to do things that take your mind off whatever is causing the stress.

Striking a balance between responsibility to others and yourself is vital to reducing stress levels.

9. Be mindful and exercise mindfulness

Stopping short of sitting astride a mountain peak in Tibet wearing some pastel flowing robe you picked up at the local bazaar, you can practise mindfulness and meditation anywhere, at any time. Put in the earbuds and listen to Zen music – if that's what rings your bell – or heavy metal music. Listen to an audio book, or pick up an actual book and lay on the grass in the shade (or sun in winter) and read.

Go get a massage. Do some breathing exercises. Practise yoga or tai-chi. Stare at a passionfruit for an hour or so. Whatever you do and what it means to you is perfect. Research has suggested it can be helpful for managing and reducing the effect of stress and anxiety.

10. Get some good sleep

Sleep is critical. Whilst research suggests eight hours of sleep every night (or day for you night shift workers) is ideal, from my experience, it depends on the individual. Whether your optimum sleep time is 6, 7, 8 or more hours per day, it's the quality of the sleep that counts. Have you ever had a long night of sleep yet woken exhausted? (No early parenting cop outs here please).

If you're drinking coffee, tea or other caffeine drink and having difficulty getting good quality sleep, you can try reducing your caffeine intake – or at least change when you drink it. Try to avoid caffeine drinks after about 2pm.

Try to avoid too much 'blue' screen time before bed. Your mind becomes stimulated by screen time and can take a lot of shutting down for sleep to kick in.

If you find yourself waking through the night as your brain decides to solve all the world's problems rather than let you sleep, try writing down a list of things on your mind BEFORE you go to bed. By transferring these thought inducers to paper, your sub-conscious will think it's already taken care of – and let you sleep. If you can't be bothered to get the pen and paper, then use your finger to 'write' the thoughts invisibly on your body, legs, sheets – wherever – as you lay in bed. It's the process of transferring the thoughts into letters and the physicality of writing them down that tells your mind that thought is taken care of.

Write a to-do list for the next day to help you prioritise, but make sure you put it aside before bed.

11. Don't be too hard on yourself

Understanding and accepting that you are, in fact, human and accordingly share those traits of humanship (is that a word?) means that you are not perfect. Shock... horror. As a human, you are expected to make the occasional mistake. So, get over it and move on. Accept that you are not a machine and dial down your self-expectation to a point where you strive for excellence, not perfection.

Try to keep things in perspective and don't be too hard on yourself. Look for positive things in your life.

12. Practice gratitude daily

Take the time right now... well, read this paragraph first... to think and write down three things for which you are grateful. While you are practising gratitude, it's impossible to think a negative thought or feel a negative emotion. So be serious about how grateful you are. It may be your health, family, friends, the weather, the dog, your warm coat on a cold day, a pool on a hot day. By writing down what you are grateful for, it plants it in your mind and makes it more real.

13. Get professional help

If you continue to feel overwhelmed by stress, consider getting professional help. It doesn't mean you're a failure. Many people are reluctant to ask for help because they perceive it as a sign of weakness.

In fact, it's a sign of intelligence and strength!

It's important to get help as soon as possible. Talk to your doctor – they can recommend the best treatment and may refer you for further help.

Stress is a silent enemy. Anxiety is an internally created fear campaign and a pre-cursor for procrastination and inactivity. The ability to recognise and deal with stressful situations will empower your life. And your lifestyle.

CHAPTER 10:
WHAT HELP SHOULD I LOOK FOR?

Your vision will become clear only when you can look into your own heart. Who looks outside, dreams; who looks inside, awakes.

CARL JUNG

Think of the past and look at how often you have asked for help, and how you asked. Did you find the process awkward? Did you experience a little anxiety leading up to the point of reaching out? And how did it make you feel – before AND after?

Then reflect on what sort of help you sought. For example, if you needed advice for an accounting or finance issue, you'd have called for an accountant. If it was an electrical issue, you probably reached out to an electrician. If you felt ill, you'd have called for a doctor (after consulting doctor Google, of course). There are specialists everywhere who will help with specific areas in life and business.

Most people are hardwired to want independence. They prefer to do things on their own and be perceived as independent, strong, capable, and efficient. Remember Chapter 8 when we looked at silhouette values? Asking for help often makes people feel uneasy because it denies potentially all of these silhouette values and more. Many people feel threatened somehow through the fact that they need help and also from the service provider themselves. Let alone ratcheting up the courage it takes to actually reach out and ask for support.

I was working with an international franchise recently where the franchise model was to help businesses increase their profits through creating savings in specific spending categories. The franchisee pitched to C-level executives whose role included increasing the profit margins. So, the biggest hurdle that the franchisee had to overcome was the threat that the client perceived in engaging them. They felt threatened because the service offering was what they should be doing, anyway.

Another fear of asking for help is being seen as needy. No one likes a needy person, right? People don't want to feel ashamed of their situation or come across as incompetent. Whatever they've been doing up to this point has led them to being in a position of needing help. They think that longer hours and working harder (at the same things) will avoid these feelings and get them back to success.

Then some people are fearful of feeling shunned or rejected if they ask for help. Hanging onto the threadbare notion that they are capable of doing and knowing everything. Particularly for a small business owner who sits atop the mini corporate tree, fielding every decision and shouldering every responsibility personally.

The irony is that many people out there truly want to help. It's not only their job, their business, but their passion.

Would you rather keep your independence and drown or own up to your own shortcomings and live to fight on?

When to ask for help

Before we explore the pros and cons of business coaches, mentors, consultants and advisors, it's important to realise your own position. That is, where you are and what you are doing – in business and in life. Mapping is one word for it. Measuring the pulse of you and your business. Running a health check. There are many terms for it.

Chapter 1 explored self-reflection and objectively looking at your own attributes and performance with a mind to how that is flowing through your business. To really evaluate the business health, be objective and be ready to ask yourself some hard questions. Your ability to provide and accept truth in response to the questions is more relevant.

An important part of seeking help is to first recognise that you need support and be prepared to accept any change that may result from engaging whatever help you need.

Unless you are ready for and WANT change, it will not happen – regardless of the calibre or amount of help you pay for. You must want to change to allow any magic to occur. And it may involve some hard work at first.

ACTIVITY 10: Business clarity

20 KEY QUESTIONS TO ASK YOURSELF ABOUT YOU AND YOUR BUSINESS

These questions are not meant to intrude or embarrass but are designed to:

A Give you a quick analysis of your Business
B Provide you with an opportunity to Review your Strategies
C Suggest a starting point for Improvement

How to score: 1 = needs attention, 5 = great

Please rate your business by giving each question a mark out of 5

Planning & management	Your score
1. Do you have weekly Sales Targets in place.... and are those targets being monitored?	
2. Do you know how much Revenue you need to Break-Even each week?	
3. Do you have a Business Plan... where you want to take your business?	

Staff training & development	Your score
4. Do your staff have clear (written) job descriptions?	
5. Are there regular reviews to assess their performance?	
6. Do you have a training plan for key staff?	

Procedures & internal processes	Your score
7. Is there a set procedure for answering and following up customer enquires?	
8. Are your Credit Terms clearly stated and enforced?	
9. Do you have regular team meetings?	

Marketing & customers	Your score
10. Do you know which of your products/services are the most profitable?	
11. Do you fully differentiate yourself from your competitors?	
12. Do you have a database of your regular customers?	
13. Are you happy with your current advertising results?	

Financial results	Your score
14. Are you satisfied with the performance of your business?	
15. Do you review your financial results against targets at least monthly?	
16. Do you have a 12 month Budget & Cashflow Plan in place?	

Personal goals & exit strategy	Your score
17. Do you have a Succession/Exit Plan ?	
18. Are you happy that you're building maximum saleable value in your business ?	

Personal goals & exit strategy	Your score
19. Can you take holidays without concern?	
20. Do you regularly take the time to work "on" your business?	
Overall rating (out of a maximum 100)	

Summary

I hope this helped you to evaluate the current health of your business.

If you scored less than 65, it's probably time to get some help with your business strategies

The previous activity gives you some clarity around areas of your business that may need attention.

If you scored less than 65 in the quiz, then there may be room for some help. Even if you scored over 65 but some areas scored poorly, then help in those areas might be worth looking into.

For example, if you scored low in the financial results section, then you might talk to an accountant. However, being great at accounting and numbers, an accountant may not be the most suitable help for other areas of your business. Most business owners already engage an accountant to discuss personal and business financial strategies and receive accounting advice.

But would the accountant be the most suitable person to talk to about marketing and customers? Or personal goals and exit strategy?

Many accountants set themselves up in practise and include business advice in their services, yet this usually only applies to advice centred on the financial aspects of business – the numbers.

Please don't misunderstand here. I'm all for accountants and financial planners. They are truly wizards with accounting and compliance for you and your business. But horses for courses. If you were in fear of drowning, would you call for a lifesaver or a lawyer? There are a range of different advisors for each type of help in your business and your life.

It's also important to understand what to expect from the help that you seek. If you engage a coach or a consultant, there's a fair chance that some form of assessment or diagnostic will be one of the first things they do. A business coach would usually look into the business's financials, business plans and talk to you (the owner) to work out where the business is right now. A life coach will map where you are in areas of your personal life. A GOOD business coach would do both. Whereas a consultant will look only at the specialist area in which they are engaged.

In small business, the line between personal life and business life can easily become blurred. And after reading so far in this book, you will understand that concept and by now (hopefully) be grasping the importance of mindset to a small business owner.

Throughout this book, we've drilled into various aspects of the mindset of the small business owner. And I raise mindset here again because when contemplating the concept of asking for help, having an open mind and a penchant for reality is important. If your mind is closed to the concept of change coming through help, then now is not the right time to ask for it.

Let's talk about coaching

Many people hear the term 'business coach' and instantly turn off. Perhaps the business owner feels threatened or fearful that the questions asked will be outside their comfort zone. Maybe the business owner feels that no coach can understand their business better than them. Perhaps they feel the threat that is perceived by being vulnerable and open. Or they just can't accept that a coach can help them.

OK I get it.

So firstly, let's dispel a few myths and misunderstandings:

- A good business coach absolutely won't know your business better than you – at least at the start.
- A coach won't do the work for you.
- A coach is not a consultant.
- A coach is not a mentor (but they can be).
- A coach is not a therapist or a psychologist - they can't prescribe medications.
- A coach is not a miracle worker (well – most coaches).
- A good coach will cost you money – get over it – because you'll make MUCH more in the long term.

A good coach believes you are totally capable and have all the resources inside of you to accomplish the life you want. And that's what it's all about. Your lifestyle. The business is there to facilitate the income and lifestyle you aspire to. So, does it not stand to reason that by improving yourself, the business will have a greater chance of success?

The coach does not know all the answers — you do. But they do know the questions to ask to extract the best from you. If you are committed to the process. And they may have a range of specialist providers that can be made available to you should you need – such as consultants.

So, who is business coaching for?

- You are just starting out and want to get traction as soon as possible.
- When you don't know what you don't know and want to make sure you've ticked all the right boxes.
- Perhaps the business has grown too quickly and you need help to get it back under control.
- You have been in your own business for a while and struggling to get ahead.
- You are doing okay and want to take your business to the next level (scale) but not sure how.
- You have been in business for some time and feel that the business owns you.
- You are tired and want to slow down – pull back from the business a little.
- You want to sell the business and need to get it ready for sale.
- You feel alone at the top of your business and want someone you can trust to talk to about your ideas.
- You are a franchisee and still feel alone and flat at the top of your franchise tree.
- You don't have a board of directors and need someone objective to run ideas past.

Everyone needs a coach. It doesn't matter whether you're a basketball player, a tennis player, a gymnast or a bridge player.

BILL GATES

If you have objectively and honestly said 'yes' to any of the above, then a business coach might be good for you. I say 'might', because coaching is not for everyone.

All successful business people have one thing in common – you guessed it - they have at least one coach. Premiership-winning teams have several coaches for different specialty skills and strategies. Elite athletes have a coach. Coaches have a coach. So, if it works for them, why would a good coach not work for you?

I have started many coaching engagements where we map where the business is currently and what the owner wants (really wants) from life. Often, the owner states they are doing what they love. That's why they are in this business. They feel they are ticking all the 'want' boxes already. Then we start talking. After about 5-10 minutes, we've spoken about what the owner wants to do in life. Travel? Time with the family? Read a book a week? Whatever. 90% of them then admit that they have not achieved their wants because they either can't afford it or don't have time because – you know... work.

Is the business REALLY providing for them to the level that they want? Food for thought.

Let's be clear. This is not an ad for coaching. Given the limited barrier to entry, anyone can call themselves a coach, and their specific skillset may or may not work in the coaching space. If you engaged one of the, let's say, less effective coaches in the industry, you may have had a bad experience.

But do not let that one experience taint the entire industry. We've all had a dodgy meal at some point, yet we keep on eating.

Bad coaches are present in every field and every city. Whether for your business or personal life, the quality of coaching can vary – and consequently, the results from coaching can initially appear to be ambiguous. Change is truly up to you. The coach is there to help facilitate the change by bringing out the best in you.

Consulting, mentoring, therapy or coaching?

The differences between a consultant and a coach can be a fine line. Many coaches also consult, but very few consultants will coach.

Similarly, the difference between a consultant and a mentor could be the experience that they bring to the table. A mentor will look at a project or task from the perspective of them having achieved or done that in the past themselves successfully. They rely on and draw upon their own experience to guide you in mentoring, not consulting.

Perhaps the best way to explain the difference between the helpers is through an analogy. Let's use horseriding as the area of interest.

Consultants

Consultants often won't tell you anything new. They'll tell you things you already know, but in another fashion that you may not have considered. They would normally be an expert in whatever chosen field you are looking. For horseriding, a consultant will be an expert horse person with years of experience in all things related to horseriding. They've already mastered it. They get paid to provide you with 'how to ride a horse' answers. They focus on the single issue.

Consultants are traditionally more technical and skilled in a specific area. You would engage a consultant for problems around how to do a specific task or when looking for someone to whom you could outsource that specific task. For example, an engineering consultant would advise at a technical level on specific engineering projects where the skills required are beyond the business owner's skills.

Mentors

A mentor has been there and done that. Using the horse riding example, the mentor has been riding horses for quite some time and is there to share their experience. They would spend time in the saddle with you and tell stories of how they became as skilled as they are, sharing their own journey. Similar to learning by seeing. They most likely have had similar problems or faced similar roadblocks as you face now.

The motivation that you take from a mentor would be based on the experience and success that they have had on their own journey. If you are in a specific industry, then the mentor that you would look to for guidance would have an abundance of

198

experience in that specific industry as well. They may or may not be classically trained and formally qualified, but they have enjoyed experience and success in the field in which you are now making endeavours.

Therapists

A therapist is most interested in whatever fears, anxiety and phobia might be the reason you cannot ride a horse. A therapist would look at what's in your past or childhood that presents a barrier to your learning? They'll hold regular sessions where they dig in to your past and work with you to fix it. They focus on why the problem is there.

Because of the technical and specialised nature of therapy, a therapist would be medically trained or specifically qualified for a psychological or psychiatric skill. Traditionally, a therapist would dig deeper and focus on one specific issue or blockage that you're facing. Then identify something in your past life that would cause any fears, phobias or anxieties that you are experiencing now.

We know that what affects the business owner often impacts the business. So, utilising the right therapist can help the owner and will, in turn, help the business. For example, if the owner's fear of conflict is impacting the business (and it usually will), then therapy to overcome that fear will flow into the business.

Coaches

A good coach will bring your skills and potential to the surface. A coach offers a different type of relationship. There's generally a lot of asking and not as much telling. Two ears and one mouth is a popular coaching phrase. They are your champion. Your rock.

They will listen to you at an intimate, honest and vulnerable level, asking questions that will get you to think along the right pathways. A coach will run alongside of you holding the horse calm and steady while you're learning. They're your cheer squad and your critic. Seeing you into success. A coach focuses on you.

Positive change is about commitment

A business owner needs to be committed to the process of positive change and be prepared to get outside their comfort zone to achieve growth and results. Having a vision is a start.

Having the conviction that change will happen and you can (to a degree) control change through your actions takes commitment. Then you seek the right help to assist with the transitions from action to action, change to change, until the goal is achieved.

With the right help for you on board, the only thing that will stop you from making your business reach the heights that match your vision of success – is YOU!

Regardless of the type of help used, a business will benefit only when the owner is committed to the process. And this commitment needs to be tangible. It needs to mean something to the recipient of the help. So whether it's a commitment of money, time, resource – whatever – it needs to have meaning.

It's very easy to SAY we are committed to a process. But when asked to make an uncomfortable decision or take an action that doesn't fall within the normal comfort zone, that commitment is put to the test. And often it's found wanting.

The achievement of goals, particularly larger, ambitious goals, takes commitment. It takes dedication and a desire to change. Without the devotion to take the necessary actions and stay focused on the objective, we, as humans, can become easily distracted. As a result, the goals can take a backward step and then always seem to appear on the horizon.

Keep going; success is right around the corner!

CHAPTER 11: SUMMING UP AND

WHAT'S NEXT

If you can't fly, then run.
If you can't run, then walk.
If you can't walk, then crawl.
But by all means, keep moving.

MARTIN LUTHER KING JR

Over the past ten chapters, we've looked at a range of different aspects of small business ownership, running, startup and a lot of mindset. We've explored what it's like to be in business, successful or struggling. We've looked at the isolationist view from the top when you go it alone and the difference it makes to your perspective when you surround yourself with the right influences. We've done some activities to help you through specific aspects of mindset and small business ownership.

Most of all, we've looked inward.

Relate this to your own experience. As a part of introspection, think from inside and look objectively at you, your business and your life, then ask yourself, 'Am I on track? If I continue down the current pathway, will it lead me to where I truly want to be?' And be objective, honest, vulnerable, and truthful with your answer. Take the time to listen to what other people are telling you. Listen to what the market, your market, is saying. Recognise indicators that will tell you, like a barometer, where you are on the success scale in business and life. Be prepared to understand the unbiased opinion about where you are right now.

So, now what to do?

In creating a plan to move forward, it's important not to focus on, but to glance now and then at where you've been. To recognise your wins and celebrate them. You can look back at any chapter anytime and reread all the content. I would really encourage you to do that because things change in business and in life. And your acceptance of change and willingness to plan and create actions to facilitate change in the right direction are key and paramount to the success that you will feel as a business owner.

But change can be difficult.

The easy option for you is to do nothing different from what you've been doing up until reading this book. And as we've discussed, the easy option is what your brain will default to. Putting yourself outside your own comfort zone is not always an easy process and can cause discomfort. But, if you've learned anything from this book, I would love it to be that the right actions will bring about change to keep you steering in the right direction for your life.

Let's look briefly at what the chapters held for you and what we've covered.

Chapter 1 was about **self-reflection and introspection.** We looked at how important it is in small business to be objective and honest in your appraisal of how the business and you are performing in line with goals and targets. Particularly when you've been going for a short while and feeling a little blocked or overwhelmed.

We looked at how self-reflection can help. And then we looked at the early stages for a business owner, focusing on mindset and the changes you need to make to succeed in that transition from startup to established.

Some challenges around establishing a business personality that lines up with your values and personality as the business owner. The different mindset cycles that can happen with a small business start-up and then running successfully as the owner transitions through the stages of the business.

Changes. In particular, small changes and how important small change and acceptance of change are to any business. Then we looked at some tips on how best to adapt to small changes in a small business.

Chapter 2 explored **mindset** and the small business owner. We looked at what mindset is – by definition and in real life, and its importance in steering our next actions. Negativity and negative language, understanding that the more negative language we use, the harder it is to move forward.

Mindset from the perspective of a growth mindset versus a fixed mindset. Negative and positive. It's true that decisions made from a negative mindset will often create negative results.

Ways to overcome negativity and negative emotions, looking at mindset change in line with business success. Negative emotions usually stem from a limiting decision made around an event or an occurrence in our past.

To finish the chapter, we looked at ways to change from a negative to a positive mindset.

Chapter 3 we explored **procrastination** and decision-making. We looked into the causes and consequences of procrastinating and delaying important decisions in business and life. How putting things off can affect a business at every level, and how we can avoid the pitfalls of procrastination.

We looked at bad decision-making and how increasing the options increases the success of a decision for a small business owner.

There are many reasons and causes for procrastination, all of them valid and all of them real. So, understanding the root cause of procrastination and taking action to get around it is an important part of developing and growing within a business.

For example, strive for excellence rather than perfectionism. Rather than worry about the outcome of a decision, research and back yourself and learn from any consequences.

Chapter 4 looked at **motivation** and action. How motivation is a mindset. There is an important relationship between motivation and action. A symbiotic type of connection where one can't happen without the other.

We looked at the different types of motivation. Toward motivation and away motivation. Exploring how we are drawn towards something we want or away from something we don't want. And these are powerful motivation aspects worthy of your understanding.

How motivation precedes every action. And how long-term motivation might stay in your mind, driving you forward, yet instant motivation will dictate the next action that you take. If we can align those two – the long-term (goal driven) motivation and the short-term (action) motivations – and get our actions stepping you towards your long-term goal, then that goal becomes so much more achievable.

The motivation of a business owner from start-up, through infancy, to the maturing of the business. How every startup is motivated by the owner's vision in a successful business. Then we explored how motivation can become a challenge when times in business get tough.

The cycle of motivation. Motivation > Action > Change > Result. And how actions lead to change and the change leads to a result, which in turn leads back to motivation.

And finally, we looked at techniques that you can use to maintain (or reclaim) your motivation when it weakens.

Chapter 5 explored the **impact of peers** and how they could be the wind beneath your wings or a deadly downdraft – dragging you down.

We looked at your core influencers and the difference between them and the community that surrounds you, imparting a different type of influence. Your core influencers include family and close friends and will be there regardless of what you do or how you do it. They're your constant, whilst your community will come and go according to what you're doing at the time they're in your life.

The power of your group and how important having the right surrounding influences is in making decisions. Having support to steer you and your business in the direction that you want.

The optimum size and structure of different groups and how social media has impacted the size and nature of our community, our tribe. We also explored how negative influencers can detract from our vision and cause blocks for forward momentum.

Chapter 6 explored goals and **goal setting.** How to create a successful goal that has a greater chance of achievement.

We looked at the IMSMART method for goal setting. For a goal or target to have the greatest chance of success, it must be inspirational, motivational, specific, achievable, risky, and tangible. The tangibility of your goal will form the measurement to tell you when it has been achieved.

The importance of setting goals and targets to give small business owners direction and motivation. To increase their chances of taking their business from infancy to success. To enable and empower themselves in their lives to achieve what they truly want.

Without setting goals in the IMSMART format, we can find ourselves adrift with no target to look at. We'll have a rudder but no compass.

Chapter 7 explored the concepts of **Cause** and **Effect**. In the context of control within your life and your business, being at Cause or being at Effect can have a massive impact on your success and achievement of goals.

When you live at Cause, you have control. You are driving and steering your own life towards your own destination. You take responsibility for everything that happens to you and with you rather than blame other people. Or events.

When you're living on the effect side of the pendulum, you will find excuses for things that go wrong, and you'll blame other people, other things and externalise the reasons for whatever is going wrong. Being at Effect creates challenges and blockages that will stop you from achieving the goals and targets you want for your life and business.

We looked at the reasons for, and the potential consequences of, living at Cause or living at Effect. We explored the vacuum created for a small business owner where they are not taking responsibility, or at least sufficient responsibility, and controlling their decisions within the business.

Finally, we looked at tips and techniques by which you can maintain your life on the cause side of this equation.

Chapter 8 looked at your **values** and how they reflect through your business. We explored the golden values, which are those outward values we want everybody to see. Happy, smart, integrity, and so forth.

We then looked into what we call our silhouette values. These are the secret values that we all have inside of us that demand to be satisfied but are usually repressed throughout maturity and development in society. Emotions and values such as feeling needy or the need to be loved. Perhaps the need to feel valued or wanted.

We looked at how you can identify your real values and how important it is to understand and recognise those to create success and align your values with those of your business. The importance of ensuring the core staff and support network share some common values to create an alignment for success of the business as a harmonious unit.

Chapter 9 explored **stress** and **anxiety**, common in small business ownership. We explored the differences between stress and anxiety, how one is based on a fear from a past event and the other is based on an event that has not yet happened.

We also identified some of the science behind stress and the brain and body responses (for those people who may understand

Klingon). The science and biology are real and tangible because chemical reactions happen inside our body when our brain detects stress.

The incidents of stress and the symptoms can be wide and varied. However, if the stress or the source of the stress is not identified and resolved, the long-term ramifications to our health and wellbeing can be significant.

We looked at a few simple ways to help reduce stress.

I emphasise if you're feeling any symptoms that you can't write off as normal in your life, lifestyle or business, then please consult with a medical professional. The tips and techniques in this book are not medical advice and under no circumstance should be used for self-diagnosis, nor treatment for stress-related conditions.

Chapter 10 looked at the type of help that you can get for yourself and your business once you recognise the type of problem and the type of help that would best fit you and your business.

We explored coaching, business coaching, mentoring, consulting, and therapy. Understanding the differences between these types of help can play an important role in getting the right type of help.

And a reminder about Chapter 1 for your objective and honest self-reflection of yourself and your business. To evaluate where you are right now is an important part in deciding the best type of help that you could get for yourself now and in the future.

Next steps

Look at where you are and what your objectives are. Then, using the information, insights, tools, and techniques in this book, I sincerely hope you and your business can thrive and achieve the heights you aspire to.

What we've done in this book is a small part of running a business of any size. There are many more facets to business ownership, such as sales skills, marketing, operations, delivery, purchasing, suppliers, expectations, staffing, outsourcing, strategies and much more.

And the truth is that owning and operating a small business is an accomplishment. It was an achievement in itself that you made the effort to start and keep it going. You are to be congratulated.

When you feel overwhelmed with how much there is to do, reflect on your capabilities and capacities, and learn how to use your strengths as your superpowers. Through reflection and self-awareness, turn your past wounds into strengths, and shine your light for others to follow.

Remember that whilst your mindset is an important aspect to success in business and life, as I just explained, there's a lot more.

And I am here to help.

I'd love to get your feedback and comments on this book and suggestions for my next one. And I'd love to hear your story and successes. If you're happy to share, we can use your story as an example to others for the empowerment of problem solving and progress.

ABOUT THE AUTHOR

Warren Ratliff is a business coach, a life coach and a small business consultant with over 30 years experience in small business.

Warren helps people and businesses change in order to be able to achieve their goals.

The first step in any transformation is identifying areas of less confidence and accepting help as you need it. I hope this book helps you with your own transformation and clarity.

Reach out if you need help or would like to share your story and feel free to share this book with anyone that you think may benefit from reading it.

WWW.PART3.COM.AU

www.ingramcontent.com/pod-product-compliance
Ingram Content Group UK Ltd.
Pitfield, Milton Keynes, MK11 3LW, UK
UKHW020143250726
13967UKWH00002B/843